CW01654823

Emissary of Light

EMISSARY OF LIGHT

MY ADVENTURES WITH THE SECRET PEACEMAKERS

JAMES F. TWYMAN

WARNER BOOKS

A Time Warner Company

DOUBLEDAY DIRECT LARGE PRINT EDITION

This Large Print Edition, prepared especially for Doubleday Direct, Inc., contains the complete unabridged text of the original Publisher's Edition.

First published by Aslan Publishing 1996.

Throughout this book some names and personal descriptions have been altered in order to respect the privacy of the people involved.

The Peace Seeds, found at the beginning of each chapter, are the shortened versions of the twelve prayers for peace offered in Assisi, Italy, on the Day of Prayer for World Peace during the United Nations International Year of Peace, 1986.

Warner Books is not responsible for the delivery or content of information or material offered by the author and other sources listed on page 394.

Copyright © 1996 by James F. Twyman
All rights reserved.

Warner Books, Inc., 1271 Avenue of the Americas,
New York, NY 10020

A Time Warner Company

ISBN 1-56865-660-2

This Large Print Book carries the Seal of Approval of N.A.V.H.

To the One in the Center

Contents

Introduction

"All my life I have been haunted by God." I remember the first time I heard my friend Lisa Wagner say those words. It was during her one-woman play about the life of Dorothy Day, and it exploded within me: I too had been haunted by God. As a small child I felt a mysterious, passionate longing for the Divine. I thought mystical experiences were natural, that everyone was having them, and because my roots were deeply embedded in my Catholic upbringing, it seemed I had but one recourse. A month after graduating from high school I joined a monastery. I would become a priest and devote my life to prayer and silence, seeking some sort of mystical union with my Beloved. I had dreamed of that day for many years, and when the huge iron gate closed behind me I knew I had crossed over to a new world.

But the empty stillness of the ancient rituals echoed within me and left me cold. Whatever it was I was searching for, I wasn't going to find it in the magic formulas and dogmatic insistence of any institution. I had to leave, to search on my own. I was like Siddhartha leaving the ascetics, or the Buddha leaving his father's palace. Even if I had to wander alone, it was my heart I would follow, and no one else's.

I have always been a man of paradox. As a child I was the black sheep, either praying in church or serving detention after school. Though I have been blessed with many gifts, I believe my greatest attribute is that I am common, ordinary. I am no smarter, no taller, no more special than anyone. The one thing that has set me apart is my desire to serve—to be an instrument of Peace. St. Teresa of Ávila once referred to herself as a broom kept in the corner of the room. Whenever the floors became dirty she was ready to be used, a tool in the hands of God.

I lived and worked in Chicago with homeless men and women living with AIDS. This is how I was used. This is when I began to feel myself moving once again back to my source, the place I felt when I was a child, and that had haunted me ever since.

Several years ago I decided to apply my lifelong gift for music to my spiritual quest. I wanted to be like St. Francis, a homeless, penniless troubadour singing about Peace. There was no way I could have known that this would bring me closer to my real mission than I could ever have imagined. This is the true story of an incredible adventure. It begins in the winter of 1994. I was living in a spiritual community dedicated to studying *A Course in Miracles*—a book that had changed my life. As for me, I do believe in miracles. Perhaps that is why this adventure found me.

Prayer of St. Francis

*Lord, make me an instrument of
your peace.
Where there is hatred . . . let me sow love.
Where there is injury . . . pardon.
Where there is doubt . . . faith.
Where there is despair . . . hope.
Where there is darkness . . . light.
Where there is sadness . . . joy.
O Divine Master,
grant that I may not so much seek
To be consoled . . . as to console,
To be understood . . . as to understand,
To be loved . . . as to love,
For it is in giving . . . that we receive,
It is in pardoning, that we are pardoned,
It is in dying . . . that we are born to
eternal life.*

AUSTRIA
HUNGARY
SLOVENIA
Zagreb
Trieste
CROATIA
Rijeka
BOSNIA-
HERZEGOVINA
SERBIA
Sarajevo
Split
Mostar
ADRIATIC SEA
Medjugorje
ITALY
ALBANIA
GREECE

ONE

The Call

Hindu Prayer for Peace

Oh God, lead us from the
unreal to the Real.
Oh God, lead us from darkness to light.
Oh God, lead us from death to immortality.
Shanti, Shanti, Shanti unto all.
Oh Lord God almighty, may there be peace
in celestial regions.
May there be peace on earth.
May the waters be appeasing.
May herbs be wholesome, and may trees
and plants bring peace to all. May all beneficent beings bring peace to us.

May thy Vedic Law propagate peace all through the world.
May all things be a source of peace to us.
And may thy peace itself, bestow peace on all, and may that peace come to me also.

—The Peace Seeds

It went off inside me like a bomb. It wasn't until I looked back months later that I realized how many seemingly unconnected events it had taken to bring me to Bosnia. We never notice them in the moment when they're happening. A chance meeting is dismissed as a coincidence. A tiny wisp of a thought inspires still more thoughts, setting into motion a whole chain of new possibilities. Months or even years go by before all the pieces fall into place to reveal the grand scheme. I felt like I was set up in some strange, cosmic way. When it was over and

I was able to look back, it was easy to see the chain of inspired circumstances.

One day my friend David gave me a sheet of paper containing the peace prayers from the twelve major religions of the world. David said he had gotten it from a place called the Peace Abbey outside Boston. I wasn't sure why he gave it to me, but I remembered him saying that he felt inspired to. Regardless of how he felt, I didn't even read them. As soon as I got back to my room, I opened my desk drawer and threw the sheet on top of all the other papers I wasn't interested in. A month later David and several other friends moved back to Boston. There was talk of starting a spiritual community in the area, and though I had never been to New England I felt a strong desire to visit my friends. I decided I would spend the first two weeks of April with them, then take a train to Florida for a week in the sun.

As I packed my bag for the trip I came across the twelve peace prayers. I sat down in the chair and began to read the Hindu Prayer for Peace. "Oh God, lead us from the unreal to the Real. Oh God, lead us from darkness to light. Oh God, lead us from death to immortality. Shanti, Shanti, Shanti unto all." As I read these words I felt a strange sensation. It was as if I could hear music, as if the prayer were being sung to me. I picked up my guitar and played what I heard. It was beautiful. The song was writing itself. I had been a performer and songwriter for years but had never had an experience like this before. When I finished I began reading the Buddhist Prayer for Peace. Once again I heard the music. I listened to each one and wrote down what I heard. It was an invigorating, energizing experience. Before I knew it, all twelve prayers were completely arranged. Not one of them took more than ten minutes. I knew something incredible had just happened. My life would never be the same.

When I arrived in Boston I asked David to take me to the Peace Abbey. The Abbey was actually a retreat center as well as a school for children with developmental disabilities. In 1986 one of the students had died and Lewis Randa, the director of both the Peace Abbey and the Life Experience School, promised to bring the child's ashes to Assisi, Italy, the home of St. Francis. By coincidence, there was a historic conference taking place in Assisi when he arrived. For the first time in history, the leaders of the twelve major religions of the world had been called together to pray for peace. Lewis was so inspired by what he saw that he brought the Peace Prayers back to the United States. The same prayers I had arranged to music had come from that meeting.

Every morning the children at the school gathered for a special prayer service. I called Lewis the day I arrived in Boston and explained what had happened. He invited me to sing two or three of the prayers the next morning. When I arrived I immediately felt at home. We gathered around a huge rectangular table that had the names of famous peacemakers engraved on its side. The service began with the children passing a copper basin filled with water around the table and washing one another's hands. They then read the names on the side of the table. Some could barely pronounce the words, but there was a feeling of grace in the room I cannot explain. Lewis then introduced me and I sang two of the prayers. No one moved. It was a holy moment. We all knew I was called to this place. I also knew that I wouldn't be leaving at the end of two weeks.

In December of that same year I was commissioned "Peace Troubadour" by Lewis and the children at the Abbey. I agreed to dedicate my life to sharing these beautiful prayers and music. Over the next year I was to travel throughout the United States performing the Peace Concert. A CD had just been released and I was preparing for a long tour. The initial plan was to perform at churches and universities in the United States for six or eight months, then spend the summer touring Europe. It was my idea to add Bosnia and Croatia to the itinerary. I felt that the "Peace Troubadour" should be willing to go where peace was needed. I didn't know if I could get into the area or, if I did, where I would perform. I had been asked to sing at a rally commemorating the thousandth day since the siege of Bosnia-Herzegovina and Croatia, and I had a burning desire to sing the Christian and Muslim Peace Prayers wherever I could throughout the Balkan region.

I admit that I knew very little about the politics of the Balkan war. Like most Americans, I knew that the former Yugoslavia was in turmoil, and that the people of Bosnia and Croatia were fighting for their lives. I wasn't sure who they were fighting, though. The news reports I occasionally glanced at were sketchy at best. The suffering seemed immense, and that's why I wanted to go. I made a conscious effort not to involve myself in the political drama, believing it would help me remain impartial and nonjudgmental. War is never about religion, of this I am sure. Religion is about peace, and I see music as a way people can understand this. I decided to begin contacting peace organizations in both countries and search for a sponsor. I mailed information with my request to every humanitarian organization in the Balkan region, about one hundred and fifty in all. Then I waited.

Months went by with no reply. I had already booked performances in Germany and Italy but kept two weeks open at the end of the tour in case anything happened. An actress friend from Chicago was performing in a one-woman play throughout Europe during the same time I would be there. We were both scheduled to perform at an international peace convention in Assisi. She gave me several leads for other possible concerts in case nothing developed in Croatia and Bosnia. By early May, during final preparations for the tour, I had nearly given up hope. I was to leave in two weeks and had assumed by then that Croatia and Bosnia would not be on my schedule. After spending time in Germany I would take a train to Italy and spend three weeks in Assisi. This alone was a dream come true. Not only was it the town where the Peace Prayers were originally prayed, but I had wanted to make a pilgrimage to the home of St. Francis my entire life. When I was eighteen I had entered the seminary and begun studying to be a Franciscan priest. I left after only two years, but my love for St. Francis, the "Poverello," never died. I was scheduled to speak and perform at the international Pax Christe convention in Assisi, then stay for an additional two weeks and perform several concerts. Since it seemed I would not be going to the former Yugoslavia I decided to stay in Assisi for an additional month to pray and reflect. I was offered a small chapel in which to conduct a peace meditation every afternoon. This new plan was fine.

That's when the fax came. Three days before I was to leave the United States, a peace organization in Croatia responded to my request. The English was broken but clear: "We would like you to come our town Rijeka to sing songs of peace. We need much peace here. Can you arrive middle June? Suncokret, Sunflower in English, is humanitarian organization to pay all expenses. We hope you come. Your friend, Gordana."

I immediately faxed a reply: "I would love to come." It did mean, however, that I would have to change my plans. I decided to spend three weeks in Assisi, travel to Croatia for two weeks, then return to Assisi. I looked on a map and found Rijeka. It was the third-largest city in Croatia, very near the Italian border. A great deal goes into planning a concert tour. But there was no information at all about where I would stay or where I would perform. The reply I sent requested more information before I left the United States. I also included a fax number in Assisi in case we weren't able to communicate within three days. I received no reply, and I left for Europe hoping the rush would not change Gordana's request. I kept reminding myself to be patient.

After a short swing through Germany I left for Assisi. I boarded a train and left Munich at around four o'clock, sharing a cabin with two young Italian men. Their English was barely intelligible, and the three of us had great fun trying to communicate. A friend had given me an Italian phrase book before I left the United States, and we fumbled through it nearly the entire night. By the time I arrived in Assisi the next morning I had only slept a few hours, but I was far too excited to care. Italy was as beautiful as I had always imagined. The train rolled past countless valleys and hills, all with quaint towns and villages nestled romantically in every corner. The train station was located in the valley below Assisi. A bus regularly took passengers from the station up the winding narrow road that led up Mount Subasio. Assisi was built on the side of the mountain, its ancient stone walls beginning at the crest of a hill, reaching down to enclose the most mystical place I have ever seen. The bus dropped me off at the town's main gate. These were the walls that protected Assisi in ancient days. They were now a reminder of a time long past, the days when St. Francis himself patrolled the area in full armor to defend his town from neighboring Perugia.

Nearly everything in Assisi was preserved to recall that time. Aside from the hotels and tourist traps, Assisi has remained what it has been for more than eight hundred years—a spiritual masterpiece of simplicity and compassion. I spent the first week within the walls of the town performing for the Pax Christe convention, and the next two weeks a few minutes down the mountain at San Masseo, an eleventh-century monastery that had been transformed into a center for young people interested in the Franciscan lifestyle. I learned of San Masseo from a chance meeting with a man in Munich. He noticed the Franciscan cross I was wearing and asked me if I was traveling to Assisi. When I told him I was, he wrote down the address of San Masseo, then the names of the two priests who live there: Father Joe and Father Paul, both Americans. As many as one hundred people stay at San Masseo each week in the summer. Mornings are spent in common prayer, then working in a nearby olive orchard. Afternoons are normally spent in silence and prayer.

During my stay at San Masseo I met a handsome Italian man named Giovani. He was a devotee of Maher Baba, an East Indian avatar who had a great love for St. Francis and who had come to Assisi to sleep in the secret cave St. Francis often used as a hermitage. Giovani knew the path that led to this cave and took me there one afternoon. It was barely large enough for the two of us but we sat inside praying for nearly an hour. Being in the cave that St. Francis had used as his hermitage was an incredible experience for me, and I decided that if I had the opportunity I would sleep there alone at least one night. Giovani and I then climbed to the top of Mount Subasio. As we sat at the crest of the highest hill, billowing clouds completely engulfed us. I felt like we were in a whole new world—that is, of course, until the clouds suddenly grew dark and I heard a low rumbling sound. Without warning we were in the midst of an unbelievable hailstorm. The small pieces of ice stung as they hit our skin. We began to run, then stopped when we realized where we were—at the top of a mountain. There was nowhere to go. The ice then turned to rain and we had a marvelous three-hour walk down the mountain, soaked to the bone.

The fax number I had sent to Gordana

was for a convent in Assisi of American nuns. The director was a friend of a friend, and she agreed to take my messages. Every day I stopped by, and every day Sister Rozita greeted me at the gate. "Nothing today. Sorry, Jimmy." When I moved down the hill to San Masseo it was a bit harder to stop by. People very naturally build up leg muscles living in Assisi. It was no more than a half mile from San Masseo to the city gate, but it was all uphill. I began to think the invitation to Croatia had been withdrawn. There hadn't been enough time to arrange things properly. Though I had been excited about the possibility of the Croatian-Bosnian part of the tour, I was also happy to stay in Assisi. I once again began making plans to stay an extra month.

I was cleaning the toilets in the men's dormitory when Father Joe called me. I had a telephone call. It was Sister Rozita: A fax had come from Croatia. When I arrived at the convent Sister Rozita was waiting at the gate. The fax was from Gordana. Preparations were being made and government permission had been granted. I was to leave by train in two days.

It took a full day to travel by train to Trieste, on the border of Italy and Slovenia. From Trieste it was an hour-and-a-half bus ride to Rijeka. It took a while to find the bus terminal, even though it was right across the street from the train station. Unlike most Europeans, Italians don't feel a particular need to learn anyone else's language. In this respect they're similar to Americans. The joke was that while traveling through Europe I quickly discovered that the meaning of the English words *a little* is relative. When asking a German if they speak English they will usually say "a little," then proceed to speak better than most Americans. When asking the average Croat if they speak English they will say "a little," then demonstrate excellent diction and grammar. But when you approach an Italian and say "*Io non parlo italiano. Parla English?*" you will of course hear "a little," just as with the others. Upon further examination, however, I often discovered something different: The words *a little* are the only English words in their vocabulary. Beyond that, hand signals are much more effective.

The bus was crowded but not full. Beside me sat a young twenty-something dark man. He was tall and rough looking, and at first I was intimidated by him. In the seats to our right sat a young, attractive blond woman. Behind me was an elderly, stout white-haired man who seemed ready to talk. He and the man beside me were already involved in some light conversation. The young woman sat looking out the window, uninvolved. She seemed scared and isolated. After a short while the man beside me said something in Croatian. I told him I was an American and didn't understand.

"Oh, an American," he said, suddenly very excited. "Where in America are you from?"

"Originally Chicago," I told him.

"Oh, Chicago. Michael Jordan. The Bulls. One of our great Croatian players is a Bull. Do you know Toni Kukoc?"

"I don't know him personally, but I've seen him play." This was exactly what I needed. I am an avid Bulls fan, and talking about my team helped me relax. I also discovered that Croats are almost as passionate about American basketball as Americans themselves.

"I am from Virginia," the old man said with a thick Croatian accent. "This is first time in twenty-five years I am returning to my homeland. I am a shipbuilder and now an American citizen. But I have many relatives still here in Croatia that I haven't seen in many years. With this war things are very different and I am not sure what has happened to them all." He turned to the young woman. "Where are you from?" he asked in English.

"Sweden," she said, then turned away.

"Sweden?" the old man continued. "Americans and Swedes all on a bus to Croatia . . . maybe to get shot. Why do you go to Croatia?"

"My boyfriend lives in Zagreb."

"I hate Zagreb," the man beside me said. "I am going back to my home. It is very near the area held by the damn Serbs. I hate the Serbs. If I could I would kill them all. I was a soldier and killed many. It is no big thing here to kill. Everyone is used to death. You sit in a café and someone throws a bomb. *Boom!* Ten people dead. This happens every day. I was in Italy for six months working on a cruise ship. But now I am going home. If the Serbs come to my town I will kill them all. You do not understand this unless you are from Croatia. This war has been going on for much more than four years. The hatred between the Croats and the Serbs goes very far back. There is no way peace will come easy."

Though I was startled by his violent attitude, I knew that this was an opportunity to learn about what was happening here. Perhaps I could get at least a fundamental grasp on who was fighting and what this war was all about. I asked him to explain.

"It's very simple," he said. "The Serbs are bastards. They think any town that has Serbian people, even if they are the minority, belongs to Serbia. If that town is in Bosnia, okay. If it is in Croatia, okay. None of this matters. If you are not Serbian you must leave. If you don't, you die. The Bosnian Serbs are people who have lived in Bosnia for a very long time but are Orthodox Christian, not Catholic or Muslim. Therefore they think they are Serbs. They don't want to be part of Bosnia, even though that is where they are. If you ask me they are all very confused. How can you be in one country but wish you were in another? There is no way for peace here. The only way for peace is for the Serbs to leave Croatia and Bosnia. If they want to be Serbian, go to Serbia. If they don't many more will die."

"But how can they do that?" I asked. "I mean, how can they tell everyone who is not Orthodox to leave just because they wish they were in Serbia?"

"Because they have the military," he said. "Before this started, Yugoslavia was the third-strongest army in Europe. When Yugoslavia broke up, Serbia kept most of the weapons. Bosnia had no weapons and no ability to defend itself. Croatia has some but not enough. In the beginning the Serbs would march wherever they wanted and kill anyone who got in their way. Now they have taken over most of Bosnia and in Croatia all the land on the border. Since Serbia had all the weapons they knew they could do whatever they wanted. Who was going to stop them? America?"

"How does religion enter into all this?"

"It does and it doesn't. Religion is an excuse to hate and kill. It has always been that way here. Croatia is almost entirely Roman Catholic, Serbia is Orthodox, and Bosnia is everything—Muslim, Catholic, and Orthodox. Bosnians have the most trouble because they are the most diverse. Nearly 75 percent of Bosnia had been taken over by the Bosnian Serbs; only 25 percent of Croatia. The religion is just an excuse. No one really cares. It is a title people carry around. They say I am Catholic, therefore I am Croatian. Or I am Serbian, therefore I am Orthodox. But none of it means anything. They just want the power and to continue hating each other." He turned to the young woman. "And you thought you were coming for a holiday."

"But the fighting is not near Zagreb," the woman said. "Is that correct?"

"That whole area is no problem," the old man said, "though it has been bombed once or twice. Just last month the Serbians bombed downtown Zagreb. Maybe five people were killed. But it is on the border of Croatia and Bosnia where they fight. Do not go anywhere near that area. It is very dangerous, especially for an American. The American government has always been on the side of Bosnia and Croatia. Russia has always supported Serbia. You must understand, Serbia never wanted Yugoslavia to break up. They wanted to remain one strong Communist country after Tito died. But it has never been one country. Even with Tito there was a clear difference between Croats and everyone else. As soon as Tito died we left, and so did the rest. Serbia is very angry and feels it has the right to take over any area it wants."

"What about Rijeka?" I asked. "How has that area been affected by all this?"

"Nothing ever happens in Rijeka," he said. "It is protected. No war ever hits Rijeka. Even when Hitler came he marched right through Rijeka. Also, because it is so close to Italy the Serbs will never touch it. To bomb Rijeka is too close to the rest of Europe. Bosnia and Croatia hope that the rest of Europe will get involved. It is our only hope because Serbia is so strong."

"Rijeka is the safest city in Croatia," the young man said. "When Croatia declared independence the Yugoslavian Army left Rijeka peacefully. In most places they destroyed many things. In every war Rijeka has not been touched. It is very strange." Suddenly his face changed and he looked very excited. "The Chicago Bulls were the greatest team ever with Jordan. Now they are nothing."

I was happy to switch back to basketball, but I had learned a lot. More than anything I learned how confusing this war was. There were the Serbs, the Bosnian Serbs, Bosnia, and Croatia, not to mention the other smaller republics aligned in one direction or the other. Everyone I met was angry at Serbia, but I knew I was only hearing one side of the story. All of this strengthened my resolve to stay out of politics and stick to music. I wasn't sure they would let me. Even this one conversation told me how emotionally charged things were. I wasn't concerned about who was right or wrong, only in demonstrating that there must be a better solution than war. But were they ready for a better solution? I began to think that they weren't. There is passion in war, even in the death and horror. Hate is a passionate emotion, and when one believes there is value in being right in a dispute, regardless of the cost, it is an emotion that is difficult to discard. Did they want to be right more than they wanted peace? The answer at that point seemed obvious.

The bus would travel across two borders. The first was Slovenia, a small country I learned very little about, and then Croatia. Crossing into Slovenia was uneventful. The bus driver stopped at the gate, signed a form, then continued on. When we arrived at the border of Croatia I could see soldiers and tanks nearby. I saw several army trucks and one tank beside a small brick building. We stopped and two soldiers boarded the bus. Their eyes were cold as they scanned the bus, then began checking passports at the front. I was nervous at the sight of the soldiers, but my friends didn't seem to care. I reached into my pocket for my passport. It wasn't there. I remembered that I had left it in my backpack, which was stored underneath the bus. I told the old man.

"This is not good," he said, quite concerned. "They are very nervous here, and they are suspicious of Americans since the United Nations arrived."

His caution frightened me. I wouldn't have thought leaving my passport in the luggage compartment was a big deal. But then again, this was my first visit to a war zone. Finally my turn came. A stern-looking man with dark eyes asked for my passport in Croatian. I asked him if he spoke English. He said, "No. Passport, please." The old man stood up and told him the situation. They talked for longer than I expected. The old man seemed to be pleading my case, and the soldier seemed to be upset.

"You must leave the bus with him," my

friend said. "They will go to the luggage with you to get your passport. I do not think there will be a problem, but he is very angry. Go and do whatever they ask."

The soldier motioned for me to leave the bus. I was escorted between both soldiers. As I stepped off, the first soldier grabbed me and forced me to turn toward the bus. He stood over me, forcing me to stay there while the other soldier walked toward a small building at the side of the road. No excessive force was used, but I was terrified nonetheless. A moment later the first soldier walked out followed by two more, one of whom was carrying an automatic rifle. The four of them stood next to the bus discussing the situation. One of the soldiers appeared to be an officer. The first two talked to him while the soldier with the gun stood silently.

"Where are you from?" the officer asked. His English was studied but clear.

"I'm an American," I said nervously.

"I am told you left your passport in the luggage. May we have a look?"

"Of course," I told him. "I have nothing to hide. I just made a mistake."

The soldier stepped back and let me turn

around. The five of us walked to the luggage compartment while the driver opened the metal door. I pointed to my backpack and one of the soldiers took it out.

"You may open it," the officer told me.

I opened the pouch and took out my passport. One of the soldiers took it.

"Would you mind opening the rest and allowing us to look?" the officer asked. His courtesy surprised me.

I told him it was fine. The first two soldiers carefully took my clothes out of the bag and examined the rest of the contents. The officer took out a pack of cigarettes and offered me one. I said no. "Please excuse this inconvenience but we must be very careful," he said. "There are many things being smuggled into this country and we are suspicious of anything out of the ordinary. Why have you come to Croatia?"

"I'm a musician and was invited by a peace organization in Rijeka to perform several concerts. I should be leaving in two weeks."

The soldiers finished their search and repacked my bag. The officer said he was taking my passport to check it and would issue me a visa. He and the soldier carrying the rifle went back to the building. The other two stayed with me. Moments later the officer came back alone and handed me my passport.

"Everything is in order," he said. "I have issued you a thirty-day visa. I hope you enjoy your stay."

I thanked him and reboarded the bus. My hands were shaking. As I sat down the man next to me laughed.

"Almost like Chicago," he said. "Croatian police are not to be played with. But if you are careful, you'll probably be okay."

"Thank you for the warning," I said.

The reality of my situation hit me. Things were different in Croatia and I had to adjust. I couldn't keep making stupid mistakes.

A half hour later we were driving through the outskirts of Rijeka. To the right I could see the Adriatic Sea. Rijeka appeared modern and well maintained. I learned that it is a major seaport famous for its shipyards. Before the war the area around Rijeka was very popular with European tourists. Opatija was one of the most famous resort areas in that part of Europe. European vacationers had stopped coming since the war began, and the economy had suffered immensely.

And yet Rijeka still appeared to be a vibrant, organized city. As the bus drove along the main road that led into Rijeka, I noticed that modern buildings and homes lined both sides. And yet so much had changed since the war. The old man told me many of these same buildings, once the posh residences of rich tourists, were now used as temporary housing for refugees and displaced persons. Even so, the people walking along the street appeared to be normal by any standard. Communism in the former Yugoslavia had been quite mild and liberal compared to the harsher policies of the Soviet Union and China. Croats were well educated and, at least before the war, well traveled.

Gordana was to meet me at the bus station. I had called her from Trieste to let her know which bus I would be on. She had sounded pleasant and excited, and I immediately had a good feeling about her. I had no idea what she had planned upon my arrival. We'd still not discussed housing or performance schedules, yet I intuitively knew everything was in order. It was clear that I would have to release my idea of how things were supposed to be done. I was happy to be on such an adventure.

The bus pulled into the terminal. I took my guitar from the rack above my head. This is how they would recognize me, carrying a guitar case covered with bumper stickers. I stepped out the door and looked for anyone who might be looking for me.

"Peace Troubadour?" The voice came from behind me. I turned and saw an attractive woman, perhaps in her early forties, with a smile that instantly made me feel welcome.

"Yes, that's me. But please call me Jimmy."

"Oh, yes. Jimmy, welcome to Rijeka. We are all so happy you came. I am Gordana. Do you have any luggage?"

"Just a backpack beneath." I walked over to where the bus driver was unloading my bag. When I turned around Gordana was standing with two other women, one of whom was holding a camera.

"Jimmy, I would like you to meet a couple of people from Suncokret," Gordana said. "This is my dearest friend, Snjezana. And this is Nela. They are both volunteers."

Snjezana threw her arms around me. "We are so very happy to meet you, Peace Troubadour," she said. "We have many things planned for you here in Rijeka."

"Nela does not speak English," Gordana said as Nela reached out her hand. "She has come to take photographs of your arrival."

I was taken by surprise. Gordana and Snjezana stood next to me as Nela took several pictures. I felt as if I was a celebrity. Before I knew it Nela waved goodbye, Snjezana grabbed my guitar, and the three of us were off and walking. I'm sure Gordana would have carried my backpack if it weren't already on my back.

We entered what I assumed was downtown Rijeka. The walkway was a closed street, constructed in a mall-like fashion. It was a drizzly evening, and the stone pavement had become quite slippery with the rain. The ladies asked me if I was hungry. I was. They suggested we go to a nearby restaurant and relax. From there we would go to a hotel where I would spend my first night. It was too late to take me to the place where they had made arrangements for me to stay.

We walked to a nice but simple restaurant just off the walkway. I ordered a vegetarian meal and my new friends ordered soft drinks. They said they had already eaten. They sat across from me and for the first time I was able to get a good look at them. They were both about the same age, attractive, and friendly. Gordana had a lovely figure with long brown hair that was pulled into a bun. Snjezana had short brown hair, glasses, and a wide, beautiful smile. What struck me the most about Snjezana was that she had a strange resemblance to my grandmother, only much younger, of course. This made me feel very comfortable. In fact I felt immediately at home with them both. Perhaps my coming to Croatia was a thing of destiny. My intuition was buzzing, but I wasn't sure why.

During my meal Gordana and Snjezana asked many questions. They wanted to know everything they could about my life, my music, and America. I in turn wanted to learn more about Croatia, but they were so inquisitive I knew my questions would have to wait. After some time the conversation turned to spirituality. It was clear that both women were very spiritual, but not religious. They were curious about my own beliefs. I told them that I was raised Catholic but had widened my vision quite a bit in the last several years. I explained that I was a student and teacher of a book called *A Course in Miracles*, which was very popular in the United States but, as far as I knew, unknown in Croatia. Neither one had heard of it. I was beginning to feel tired, so I said I would tell them all about it the next day.

We left the restaurant and walked to the hotel. The Continental Hotel was apparently one of the finest in the city, where in good times it was nearly impossible to get a room. But there were no tourists now. Gordana and Snjezana checked me in and took me to my room. After a few minutes they said they had to go home to their children. I gave them both hugs and they left, tears in their eyes. I knew what they were feeling, though I didn't understand it at the time. Something mystical was taking place, I was sure of it. But at that moment I was too tired to think about it. I took a bath and went to bed.

TWO

The Dream

Buddhist Prayer for Peace

May all beings everywhere plagued
with sufferings of body and mind
quickly be freed from their illnesses.
May those frightened cease to be afraid,
and may those bound be free.
May the powerless find power,
and may people think of befriending
one another.
May those who find themselves in trackless,
fearful wildernesses—
the children, the aged, the unprotected—
be guarded by beneficent celestials,
and may they swiftly attain Buddhahood.

—The Peace Seeds

I woke up filled with a strange energy. What had inspired me to want to come to the former Yugoslavia to perform the Peace Concert? Now that I was here I felt complete, as if I were about to fulfill some role I had been preparing for my entire life. I was still unable to understand my feelings, except that I was glad to be there.

The Continental Hotel was two blocks away from Suncokret's office. I had made arrangements to meet Gordana there at ten. Snjezana worked at a grammar school nearby and agreed to meet us for lunch. I tried to remember exactly where I was and guess which direction it would be to the office. I arrived a few minutes early and welcomed the opportunity to explore the neighborhood. The atmosphere was not much different from many European cities I had been to. Rijeka was not large by U.S. standards, but the business district was as active as in any medium-sized city. It was nestled between the Adriatic and rolling green mountains. There was no outward sign of the war, but it was the main concern of everyone.

The young people seemed no different than their counterparts in the United States. They listened to the same music and wore the same clothes. As I passed a movie theater I noticed they showed the same movies as well.

After wandering a bit, I found the office. It was located in an old building near the center of town. The building looked as if it were more suited for apartments than offices. Suncokret was the only office in the building. They had an arrangement with a young dancer who lived down the hall to use his bathroom. I walked up the worn, unkempt staircase to the third floor and knocked on the door. I heard Gordana's voice, so I walked in. The office was tiny and cramped, just large enough for three desks. Gordana sat at the middle one.

"Jimmy, my love, please come in." I walked over and gave her a hug. "Did you sleep well?" She motioned for me to sit down in the chair opposite her desk. The office had only one window, with a potted plant balanced on the sill. The walls were covered with posters and photographs.

"The hotel was wonderful," I told her. "I took a little walk to get a feel for the area."

"You'll find Rijeka a beautiful and very friendly city. Have you had coffee?"

I said that I hadn't, so she suggested we go to the café just below the office to talk. It was a beautiful day and we took a table near the sidewalk. I ordered a cappuccino. It was impossible to find American coffee in Croatia. The thick-ground coffee they served was delicious, but there were times when I would have given anything for a cup of Starbucks French vanilla.

"Please tell me all about Suncokret," I said. "What kind of work do you do?"

"Suncokret is a humanitarian organization that works with refugees, mainly from Bosnia. We have a number of programs, like housing and food. Most of our funding comes from contributors in Italy. We rent apartments, distribute food and supplies, and sometimes give workshops. You see, the stress of leaving your homeland and being forced to live in a new country is very difficult. It is often acted out in strange ways. Parents neglect their children. They neglect their health and well-being. We teach them motivational skills that give them back some hope. This is the thing they have the least of."

"Why are you interested in having me perform?"

"I'm not sure," she said. "There was something about your letter. I went to our director and told her I wanted to invite you. At first she said we didn't have the money and that this isn't what we do. But I was certain you should come, so I pressured her. Finally she agreed. I'm still not sure why, but I know it is important you are here."

"It's funny because I have the same feeling," I told her. "Long before I sent that letter I felt I had to come. I was so happy when I received your invitation. And now that I'm here I feel this even stronger."

"Some things are not for us to understand, I guess. We'll just have to wait and see."

We began discussing the schedule. Several appearances were already planned in Rijeka. I was to appear on national Croatian television the next day as part of the daily newscast. The day after that I would participate in a festival honoring St. Vida, Rijeka's patron saint. This was apparently a great honor. Several other performances and appearances were planned in both Rijeka and Zagreb, but there were no details yet. I had also been invited to perform in Sarajevo, but things were especially violent at that time and no one knew if it was possible to even get into the city. After an hour of discussion we sat back and relaxed.

"Yesterday I mentioned the book *A Course in Miracles*," I said. "Maybe now would be a good time to tell you more about it."

"Yes, now is a fine time."

I spoke for several minutes and gave a brief introduction. The *Course* had been translated into many languages, but not Croatian. As I talked, Gordana looked as if she understood what I was speaking about.

"You know, this sounds like a book a

friend gave me," she said as she reached into her bag, pulling out a pile of folders. "A friend of mine found a book in English that he liked so much he translated it into Croatian himself. He typed it, made copies, and gave them to many people. It has become a very popular book in this area, even though there were originally only about a hundred copies. Those who had copies made more. No one knew where it came from or what it was called because he didn't even include the title—and yet it caused a great deal of excitement."

I picked up the pile. There were six folders with about seventy-five typed sheets in each one. They looked very unprofessionally done. I opened to a random page and asked her what the title said.

"It says, 'I Am Under No Laws But God's.' "

I nearly fell off my chair. It was *A Course in Miracles*! She was already a student and didn't even know it. She explained that there were many in that area who were studying the book, some of whom had gathered in groups, much like in the United States. And yet there was an amazing lack of interest in the source, or even the title. They seemed content to read and experience what they were able. Gordana told me that a friend of hers once asked what the title was and she had responded without even thinking, "The Jesus Exercises." She was overjoyed to hear that I had led many workshops on the *Course*, and had even lived in a community that studied and experienced it exclusively. The pieces were beginning to fall into place. Perhaps I wasn't here as much for the Peace Concert as I had thought. The music had always been a form of teaching for me, but unless I was with a group of people that was aware and interested in the Course, I kept that part of my life quiet.

Snjezana was a student of *A Course in Miracles* as well. She was a volunteer for Suncokret primarily because of her friendship with Gordana. It was evident that their lives were clear reflections of what they believed in. They participated in prayer and meditation groups several times a week. I was amazed to discover that Croatia had many of the same groups and centers that we have in the United States. When Snjezana joined us for lunch an hour later she was thrilled by our discovery. The connection all three of us had sensed was real indeed. And yet I felt that there was something more that they had to tell me. It seemed as though there was some secret Gordana and Snjezana shared that I was not included in, but that involved me. Perhaps it was part of the drama that was beginning to unfold. Though I believed information was being withheld from me, I was not suspicious of my friends. I had no feeling of being unsafe or set up. To the contrary, I was certain this was a wonderful adventure I had chosen and was an active participant in.

After lunch Gordana and I took a bus to Suncokret's second office. It was here that most services were provided. Gordana asked me to bring my guitar. She felt it would be a nice gift to the women and children attending a workshop there. We walked to a busy bus stop around the corner from the office and a block away from the Adriatic. This appeared to be the main road leading out of the downtown area. The bus was filled, and it rounded the sharp turns precariously. As in many European cities, one does not need to show a pass or buy a ticket when boarding, though everyone is expected to have one. Now and then an officer gets on and checks. If you're caught without one you're escorted to jail. I saw this happen on my first ride. The young man was caught and he knew it. There wasn't much discussion—the bus stopped and he left with two officers. Gordana had already bought me a pass, so there wasn't much chance of getting arrested on my first day. Once again, the office was in a residential area in a building intended for apartments, not offices. We got off the bus at the street, then walked up several flights of stairs that led up a steep hill. As we walked along the sidewalk that led to the front door, I saw an old man sitting outside his door scaling fish. He smiled and nodded his head as we passed. Ahead were two women and one man, all smoking cigarettes. Gordana knew them all. I smiled and followed her through the door.

This office was bigger than the first but still quite cramped. Nearly everyone was crowded into a room no bigger than the average living room. Most of them were smoking, something I had difficulty adjusting to. It seems that this part of Europe still hadn't embraced the anticigarette movement so popular in the United States. The room was a haze of smoke and voices.

About eight children were sitting around a table working on an art project when we walked in. Five or six women stood about, talking. When they saw me the conversations stopped. Gordana spoke in Croatian, introducing me as "Jimmy, Peace Troubadour, Bostona." The women stepped forward all at once and offered me their hands. Some greeted me in English. Others spoke Croatian. They were all genuinely happy to have me there.

"You may greet the children in English, if you wish," Gordana said.

I turned toward the table. "Do you speak English?" I asked them.

At first they didn't say a word. Then Gordana encouraged them. "We speak little English from school," a little girl finally said.

"How old are you?" I asked.

"I am nine," she said.

"You know, I have a daughter back in the United States who is the same age as you are. Her name is Angela. What are your names?"

The children went around the table and told me their names. Then I asked what they were working on.

"We are making T-shirts for the St. Vida festival in Rijeka," one of them said.

"That's wonderful," I said as I shook her hand. "All of you speak English so well, better than my Croatian." The children laughed.

"These women are all working for Suncokret," Gordana said as she introduced them. As she spoke I noticed a young woman walk into the room. She didn't seem interested in me or what was happening. She went and sat down with the children.

I leaned over to Gordana. "Who is that?" I asked, pointing at the woman.

"Oh, I'm sorry. That's Nadina. She runs the crisis line for Suncokret." She turned toward the woman. "Nadina, this is Jimmy from America."

She smiled and nodded her head. Though she didn't say anything I could tell she spoke English. She was a dark, interesting-looking woman. Her hair was short and curly, and she wore a dark shade of lipstick. She had piercing eyes. I noticed this when I saw her sneaking a look at me. I smiled and she immediately turned away. Several of the other women were gathered around me asking questions. After a moment or two I excused myself and walked over to get a drink of water. Then I walked to where Nadina was sitting.

"Do you work with the children?" I asked her.

"Why do you assume I speak English?" she said with a slight bite.

"Because Gordana introduced us in English and you seemed to understand her."

"It's not hard to understand the words 'Nadina, this is Jimmy from America.' Even without English I would have known what she meant. No, I don't work with the children. They are here today because of a workshop for their mothers. I run the SOS line for people who want to kill themselves."

"I can see why that might put you on edge," I said with a smile.

"What makes you think I'm on edge? Maybe I just don't like pushy Americans."

"But why wouldn't you like Americans? And besides, what makes you think I'm pushy?"

She seemed to let her guard down. "I'm sorry. Actually, I love Americans and want to be one. I am angry because I can't leave this damn country and go where I want. You see, I'm from Bosnia. Just like these children, I'm a refugee. No one wants refugees. There are too many of us. I have put my immigration papers to the United States, Canada, and Germany, but they all say they have let in enough Bosnians. I'm twenty years old and can't go to school, can't get a real job, but I also can't leave because if I go home I will be shot. I guess this would put anyone on edge."

I liked Nadina instantly. She was honest and fiery. But I was also drawn to her vulnerability. This was a side of the Balkan war I had not seen yet. Though Rijeka was not in the path of the tanks and guns, refugees flooded in every day. And though Croatia welcomed them, they also ignored them. They were given adequate food and shelter, but in most cases were denied the things most of us take for granted. It was very difficult to get a work permit. Many Croats seemed to look down on the Bosnians just because Croatia was just a bit better off. But a refugee has little choice. Forced to leave their homes, they have little say over where they end up. For a few it is a ticket to a new life in a country that is not so apt to erupt in ethnic warfare. But for most it means living in refugee camps that offer no hope of a normal life.

Nadina was somewhat lucky in that she didn't have to live in a refugee camp. Suncokret had secured a small apartment for her family where she lived with her mother, Neda, and her brother, Ned. All three worked in some way at Suncokret. She herself responded to people calling in distress, her mother was something like an office manager, and her brother showed up when needed. I assumed that others in the office had similar arrangements. How many were from Bosnia and how many were from Croatia I did not know. I knew that Gordana and Snjezana were Croatian. They had lived in Rijeka their whole lives, neither one was currently married and each had one child, Gordana a boy and Snjezana a girl.

Gordana asked if I would sing a song for the group. They had apparently been waiting a good while already. I took out my guitar and sat down on a chair. I sang the Prayer of St. Francis, my own arrangement. The room was still. When I was finished I looked up at Nadina. She had turned away but I was sure she was crying.

"That was so beautiful," one of the women said. "You must play for us every day."

I stayed at the office for another hour. It was good to learn more about their lives. That is why I was there—to be personally involved with these people. It was already late in the afternoon and Gordana felt it was time for us to start in the direction of my new home—a dormitory above a kindergarten in Kostrena, a small town on the outskirts of Rijeka. One of the women offered us a ride. As we were leaving I turned to look at Nadina. She waved and gave a quick smile. I knew at that moment we were going to be great friends.

The kindergarten was only a block from the Adriatic Sea. Someone met us at the school and showed me upstairs. There were five rooms, each with about five beds. Though used as summer-camp accommodations, the place was empty now. Since I was able to choose whichever room I wanted, I chose the one with the best view. The room also featured a balcony that looked out over the sea. The branches of a tree filled with cherries hung over the balcony. They would make a nice breakfast, I thought. I set my guitar and backpack on my bed and walked Gordana to the car.

"This was my first full day in Croatia," I told her. "But it feels like I've been here a year."

"You were sent to us, Jimmy. I'm not sure why but I know you were. I have the feeling we're in for a great adventure."

"I have the same feeling, Gordana. But I also have the feeling you know more than you are saying. Is there something going on here that I'm not aware of?"

Gordana looked nervous, as if she were not able to tell me something she wanted to. "All I can say is this," she finally said. "It is no accident you are here . . . you! There is no one else who can do what you must do here. Beyond that I don't know anything, only that we will each be shown when the time is right."

Her words seemed ominous and a bit frightening. "I don't understand," I said. "It sounds as if you brought me here for more than just music. And yet you couldn't have known anything else about me. You couldn't have known that I teach workshops, or that I wrote a book a few years ago, or anything else about me."

"What kind of book did you write?" she asked.

"It was a spiritual novel called *Secrets of Unconditional Love*. I self-published it, so it was never a best-seller or anything."

Gordana smiled and gave me a warm hug. "I don't even know what to say. But I believe we will soon all know what to do. All I know is that I am glad you are here. When I received your letter I had the most unusual feeling, as if I already knew you. I didn't know what it meant but I knew it was important. I'm sure we will all be surprised by what will happen, but for now we must be patient."

Patience was never one of my strengths. I was intrigued by all this mystery. I wanted to know everything, but I was convinced that she had told me most of what she knew.

Gordana said goodbye and got into the car with her friend. "Come to the office tomorrow morning," she said through the window. "Snjezana is not working so the three of us will spend the day together. The television appearance is at four-thirty. *Ciao, Bok.*"

I was to learn that these last two words literally meant "Goodbye, God," a common farewell in that part of Croatia. Looking back now, it seems appropriate considering everything that was about to happen.

I went to sleep early that night. My mind was still swimming from all the events of the past two days. I had felt a powerful energy ever since I arrived in Rijeka. At first I wasn't able to determine what it was, only that I felt energized and a little disoriented. These feelings had increased that second day, especially with all the new revelations and connections I was experiencing. And then there was the fact that I was in a country at war, but had no sense of what that meant yet. I put my things in order, then climbed into the bottom bunk of a bed made for an adolescent.

That night I had an amazing dream. I was running alone through a forest, lost and running for my life. I could hear the sound of feet behind me, as if someone or something was chasing me. I was nearly out of breath. It seemed as if the footsteps behind me were getting closer. I couldn't see anything except the thick forest. I had no idea where to go.

Suddenly I had a strong feeling, almost a voice, that told me to stand perfectly still. At first I was afraid, but the feeling was so powerful that I did what I was told. I stopped and held my breath. The footsteps were coming very close. I realized that there was more than one person chasing me. Then I could see them. Five soldiers carrying rifles ran out of the brush and rushed right past me. One of them nearly stepped on my foot. And yet not one of them saw me standing there as they continued through the forest until they were out of sight.

I collapsed. I was filled with fear and couldn't move. Were they looking for me? Were there more on the way? Who were they? None of this made sense. Then I heard a faint pulse, as if my head were against someone's chest. The heartbeat grew louder around me, until I stood up and wondered where it was coming from. I looked around, sensing that everything was going blurry. But it wasn't—I realized that something very large was actually materializing right in front of me. It became clearer and clearer, until I could see the outline of a small dome house. It took about a minute to fully materialize. I stood up and walked around its periphery. I was the only one there.

I examined the structure. The base of the building was supported by twelve walls. Atop these walls was the dome, made of hundreds of wood pieces, each with exactly twelve sides. I saw a wood door on one of the sides. I walked up to it and touched it lightly. It opened.

A marvelous smell came from the inside, like earth and incense. At the top of the inside of the dome was a huge crystal pointing straight up. Around it were twelve lanterns. As my eyes adjusted to the change in light, I saw a staircase in the very center leading down into the earth. Apart from that, the room was empty. I walked over to the staircase and listened. I could hear nothing. More lanterns lit the way, so I descended the staircase. It was a narrow walk. I felt the earth walls, cold and moist. I wondered where this stairway would lead. Shortly it ended at a door made from a piece of canvas.

I pulled aside the canvas but did not enter. Before me was a huge white room, dazzling radiantly—and yet I saw no lanterns or other source of light. The size of the room was hard to gauge, but it had to be at least a hundred feet around. Like everything else in this place, the room was twelve-sided, with some sort of a diagram on the floor. The diagram began in the center of the room and extended out like the spokes of a wheel. There were, of course, twelve spokes. In the center sat a man. It looked as if he was meditating. Then his eyes opened as if he suddenly realized I was there.

"Please come in," he said, his deep voice loud enough to carry across the large space. I stepped through the doorway and approached the center. The man watched me, smiling. He was middle-aged or older, with dark, thick hair. I recognized he was an American when he spoke. Though his voice was powerful, it soothed me completely. I stepped over the thick line on the floor that seemed to enclose the twelve spokes. The spokes themselves were not lines at all but hundreds of small, ancient-looking symbols that gave the illusion of lines. I walked slowly within one of the sections until I was about fifteen feet from the man.

"Sit down on the ground," he said. "You don't have to worry, this place is very clean. Do you know why you were brought here?"

"I don't even know where I am, let alone why I'm here," I said.

"You're here to learn about peace," he said. "Not the kind of peace the world understands, but an experience of peace without an opposite. This is the Peace that cannot be found in the world but can be expressed here. It is expressed through Divine Light, or the extension of an energy that is the very foundation of life. Once you learn this, you'll teach it. That is why you were called here—because the world needs to finally understand how to create the Peaceful Kingdom, a world based on love, not fear."

"But why am I here? I mean, this is just a dream, I know that, but I also feel like I'm not asleep. You said that I was brought here. What do you mean by that? I'm here because I want to be. I asked to come to Croatia and Bosnia. No one forced me to do anything. And besides, this is just a dream, right? I'll probably wake up and forget all about this."

"Maybe," he replied calmly. "But whether you forget or not, you're here for the reason you're here, regardless of why you think you came. Everything will happen as it should. Try to relax and be patient. Everything is in order."

"What is this place?" I asked.

"This place has existed in one form or another, in one place or another, for thousands of years. It is the place of the Emissaries of Light. The wheel you are sitting on is very important because it is here that a choice is made for humanity that humanity is still unable to make for itself. This is the choice of Peace. It is from this wheel that the energy of Divine Light, or Peace, is extended through time and space. Until now the consciousness of the planet has been unable to sustain this energy field by itself. Therefore this place has existed secretly in regions of the world where the energy is most dense—the areas experiencing the most violence and discord. Now the mass consciousness is ready to shift to the next stage of evolution. This physical place soon will no longer be needed to extend Divine Light because small groups and individuals will be strong enough to do it alone.

"And this is why you are here, to experience Divine Light and learn how to extend it just as the Emissaries do. Then you'll teach what you have learned. The world is hungry for this knowledge. These secrets have already been given to certain individuals who have expressed them in different ways. Your mission will be somewhat different in that you will tell the world about us—the Emissaries of Light. It is important that people understand the choice we have made for them so that they can begin making it for themselves. Everything you need will be given to you as you need it. You were brought here because you are capable of making the shift yourself, and because you are already free enough not to be caught by the traps you will encounter."

"What kind of traps?" I asked.

"You will soon see. This is enough for now. You will remember all of this and, when the time is right, you will find yourself here again. For now, remember to be patient."

That was the last thing I recalled. I hesitate to even call this a dream, for it seemed so real. The next morning I awoke feeling refreshed and clear. I wondered if I would say anything to my friends.

The bus for downtown Rijeka stopped in front of the kindergarten. When I went downstairs in the morning the building was already filled with small children. I wasn't sure if the teachers had known I was there, as they seemed surprised to see me. I said hello and walked out the front door.

The kindergarten was on the main highway that ran along the Adriatic. I decided to take a walk to the sea before boarding the bus. The houses and small hotels I passed were quaint and beautiful. I walked down the hill for about five minutes before I reached the shore. A cement path ran alongside the shore, apparently beginning somewhere near the center of Rijeka, then continuing several miles through an area obviously meant for tourists and vacationers. I walked past several small restaurants and cafés, all with patios and outdoor tables with colorful umbrellas. Nearly all of them were empty, another sign of the slumping tourist trade. I could see why this was normally such a popular area. The water was clear and warm, while rocks and mountains rose from the sea like majestic monuments. Here and there I saw women sunbathing alone on the beach, or a lonely fisherman sitting on a rock with his line hanging lazily in the water. Otherwise the area was deserted.

I walked back to the main road and waited for the bus. Before long I was in the center of town, and as I got off the bus I saw Snjezana waiting for me. She held a basket in one hand and a thermos in the other.

"You and I are going to have a picnic breakfast," she said. "I have coffee, milk, rolls, and cheese. If you need anything more we can stop at the market."

"Wow, what a great surprise. Where will we have this picnic?"

"In the park," she said. "It is very close. Gordana must go to a meeting and will meet us this afternoon. Until then you are mine."

There was something so wonderful about Snjezana. From the first moment we met I felt connected and close to her. There was a childlike quality about her that I loved. There was also something I couldn't describe, like strength or certainty. Unlike Gordana, she was completely sure of herself. She also was not shy about expressing her feelings. And yet there was a wisdom about her that seemed timeless. I was to rely on her a great deal in times to come.

We arrived at a small park near the center of town beside a river that ran into the Adriatic. Small boats tied to posts bobbed along the shore. On one side of the river was a busy road, on the other, the park. We sat down on the grass and laid out our picnic. It was a hot and sunny day. Young people were everywhere, clumped together in small groups, laughing and listening to music. The music was American and British, and I had stopped counting how many wore Chicago Bulls hats and shirts.

"Jimmy, we want you to give us a talk about this *Course in Miracles*," Snjezana said as soon as we were settled. "There are many in Rijeka who would be very interested in this. Many people have already read the book but have trouble understanding it. We can get a large room in the center of town and put up notices. Maybe twenty or thirty people will come."

"What are they having trouble understanding?" I asked her.

"I don't know if it's the translation or what, but it is very difficult to grasp. I love the book very much but need help myself. Maybe this is why you are here, to help us learn."

We decided to have an evening talk in two weeks. I still believed I would be returning to Italy about that time, but the thought of giving a talk on the Course was very exciting. Snjezana said she would talk to the principal of the school where she worked to see if he would let us use a room. If not, Suncokret had a large empty apartment in the center of town.

"Snjezana, I had a very strange dream last night." I decided to find out exactly how much she and Gordana knew about what was happening to me. I told her my dream in as much detail as I could remember. She listened intently. When I was finished she didn't say anything for a while—she just smiled at me.

"What do you think it meant?" she finally asked.

"I have no idea. I was wondering if any of it sounded familiar to you."

Once again she sat without talking. Then she reached over and touched my hand. "Jimmy, there are many things happening in Croatia that I don't understand. A terrible war has been raging for four years. So many people have died and there is so much hatred everywhere. It is a very dark time for this country, and for the world. Perhaps this is why you are having these dreams, because of your desire to help bring peace."

"That's obviously the reason I came here," I said, "to do a peace concert. But now something else is happening. I can feel it. I'm having incredible dreams, and I also feel like you and Gordana know more about these things than you're saying. Please, Snjezana, if you have any idea what's going on please tell me."

"I know very little," she said. "All I know is that you were brought here, perhaps not for the reason you think. I know it seems like a coincidence that you are here at this time, but your coming here was arranged."

"Arranged by whom?"

"That's what I don't understand. Gordana was told to invite you by someone you'll meet later. His name is Duro. Gordana had shown him your letter, and he said that you are the one who is supposed to come to Croatia to 'Initiate the Light,' or something like that. He told Gordana that it was very important you come to Croatia. Gordana and I did not understand, but we trust Duro. He is a wise and good man. He is involved with a community somewhere in the mountains that does some special type of healing work, just like in your dream. But he did not tell us anything else about you, only to make sure you came. He will come to you when the time is right."

"So in other words, I was tricked into coming to Croatia?"

"Not really," she said, laughing. "I am sure you will do many concerts, and I am very excited about that as well. The rest will happen when it is supposed to. Then we will all understand this."

"What do you know about this community in the mountains?" I asked.

"I do not know anything. He has never mentioned it to me, only Gordana. It is very secret. No one else knows of it or where it is. Gordana told me that the meditation they do is meant to bring peace to the world; that is all I know."

I was startled by this disclosure. "Was I brought here? Who is Duro and why does he think I'm supposed to be in a war zone?" I was suddenly very afraid. Questions raced through my mind. Had I fallen in with a group of psychopaths in a country I knew nothing about? What had they planned for me? For a moment I thought about taking the first train to Rome and going home. Apart from my premonitions, I wasn't ready for this, especially if it meant being held captive in a strange and violent country.

"Jimmy, you should not worry about these

things now," Snjezana said. "In your heart you know you are safe. You know that Gordana and I will not let anything happen to you. You must trust us for now, even though we are not sure about these things ourselves. I know that there is something very wonderful about to happen, and this is all I need to know. The rest will happen when it is time."

That afternoon I appeared on a television news program. People seemed genuinely interested in my reasons for coming to Croatia, and in my music. *My music.* This is why I came, not to be pulled into some spiritual fantasyland. Though I did trust Snjezana and Gordana, I was feeling concerned. Yet I was doing exactly what I came to do. I had just appeared on national television and expressed my ideas on peace, I was booked for several concerts, and I had met some wonderful people. Regardless of what lay ahead, I was accomplishing my goals. I felt powerless to get in the way of whatever plans were in store for me.

THREE

The Way Things Are

Zoroastrian Prayer for Peace

We pray to God to eradicate all the
misery in the world:
that understanding triumph
over ignorance,
that generosity triumph over indifference,
that trust triumph over contempt, and
that truth triumph over falsehood.
—The Peace Seeds

Being a stranger in a strange land can be very exciting. On the one hand I was completely unknown; yet after appearing on national television I felt a bit like a celebrity. People noticed me on the street. I was approached more than once by someone who seemed to congratulate me for my performances, but I was never completely sure. They would smile and move their hands as if they were playing an air guitar. Without the aid of English, it was hard to tell what they were saying to me.

The next day I met Gordana at Suncokret's main office, the one I had played at two days earlier. There was less activity than before, but I soon learned businesses in Croatia are run differently than in the United States. The office was almost always filled with smoke, there were far more people than were able to comfortably fit, and office equipment was in short supply. But this, of course, was not the United States. The situation was quite different, especially since the war began. Through all the confusion it was clear that these people were committed to making an impact. Refugees in need of basic supplies filed in and out, day after day. Some needed food for their children. Others needed to have their rent paid. It was also apparent that there wasn't enough to go around. Though many were helped, others were referred to agencies more suited to their needs.

Plans were being made for two performances in Zagreb, the capital of Croatia. I had been invited to perform and be interviewed on a popular television program, as well as to perform the Peace Concert at a local Catholic Church. Nadina was asked to help with the arrangements. She resisted, but I began to suspect that this was more her personality than a statement of dislike. In fact,

I sensed that Nadina really liked me, in spite of her constant attacks on my "typical American attitude." Her fiery style was delightful, even when it was at my expense. After a couple of hours I asked her if she would join me for a cup of coffee at a café across the street.

"Why do you want to go to America?" I asked her after we were seated.

"It is not so much I want to go to America as I want to leave here," she said. "I would like to go to my own country and home, but that is impossible. I would like to have my old life back, my life before the war. I was going to college, I had many friends, and could go anywhere in Europe I wanted. It was nothing to take a train to Italy for a week. Now we are treated as if we are criminals. We cannot get a visa to go anywhere because they are afraid we will never return home. Things were better when we were Communists than they are now.

"One day I am in my home getting ready for school and there is a knock on the door. A soldier is standing there, a Serbian soldier, and he tells us we have twenty-four hours to leave this house and evacuate the city. Anyone who disobeys will be shot. My best friend, a man who lived a block away, was taken away in a car and never seen again. Anyone they suspected of trouble or nationalistic ideas disappeared immediately. I never thought such things could happen in my country. My mother, my brother, and I had to put a few things in three plastic garbage bags and leave. We had nowhere to go—no car, nothing. All Muslim people left in a big line, walking to who-knows-where.

"We hitchhiked, rode in trucks, and walked until we reached Croatia, then Zagreb. My mother was determined that we wouldn't live in a refugee camp. They are horrible, sad places. No one has any hope there. But there is very little a refugee can do in a foreign country, even when that country was part of your homeland a few years before. We stayed with a friend at first, then my mother got a job—not a legal one but one that paid cash and didn't need papers. She even got my brother and me into school. My brother went to trade school and I finished my nurse's training. It seemed as if things were finally going well. I liked Zagreb very much. I had many friends and went dancing nearly every night. But then my mother decided to move to Rijeka. I do not even know why. I had no choice but to come, even though I hate it here. There is nothing to do and nowhere for young people to go.

"If I could go to America I would go to a university and make something of my life. Things are over for me here. Even if the war were to end tomorrow things could never be the same. There is too much hate and too many wounds. A friend of mine moved to South Carolina because he has relatives there. But it is very hard to get into another country, especially America. It seems like I will never leave but will have to stay here and do nothing."

I wondered if there was anything I could do to help her. Nadina's story touched me deeply. It made me realize the privileges I have as an American citizen. Wherever I go, all I do is show a passport with the words *United States of America*, and doors open. It was hard to understand how that little booklet made me so different from Nadina. She could go nowhere. She was from a country at war, a country with hundreds of thousands of refugees just like her, people that once led normal, secure lives. Suddenly they were no longer wanted in their own towns, just because of their country's national religion.

"Maybe I can help you get into the States," I told her.

"Don't even say that," she said. "I am tired of people saying they can do this or they can do that, then doing nothing."

"I don't know what I can do. I don't know if I can do anything, but I'm willing to try. Why don't you come to Zagreb with me and we can go to the embassy together? Then we can ask them what we need."

"But you can't just walk into the American embassy and ask these things," she told me. "You have no idea how it is here. Their job is to keep people like me out, and they do it very well. They will know why I want to go, because I don't want to be here. And then they will say no. I have to be able to show them I have a reason to come back here, like children, or property, or a business."

"Maybe we can make something up," I said naively. "I'm sure that if we find out what they're looking for, and invent the circumstances that fit it, we would have as good a chance as anyone."

"Which is very little chance at all. Bosnians are rarely given visas, no matter what the circumstances."

"But we can try. Say you'll come to Zagreb with me. We can tell Suncokret that I need you to translate or something. You never know what will happen until you give it your best shot."

"That sounds so American," she said, smiling at last. "You are like John Wayne. All right, I will ask and see if I can come. At least it will be an excuse to go to Zagreb. I can show you around and we can have some fun. Now, I have a question for you: How do you like living in a kindergarten? If you want you can come and stay with my family in the center of town. My brother has an extra bed in his room. I would like to have you around more, and my mother has invited you as well."

I was thrilled with this invitation. Even though it was nice being a block away from the Adriatic, it was a bit isolated. We paid for the coffee and Nadina came with me to get my belongings.

A week later Nadina and I were preparing for our trip to Zagreb. Three French volunteers were traveling through Rijeka on their way to Zagreb with supplies for a refugee camp. They had room in their van and offered us a ride. We met at Suncokret and rearranged boxes of toilet paper and sardines in the back to make room for the two of us. Zagreb was about three and a half hours from Rijeka, so Nadina and I settled in between the supplies and prepared for a long, uncomfortable ride. Only one of the French people spoke English, and it was very little. None of them spoke Croatian. Nadina and I were left to ourselves.

"Tell me what Zagreb is like," I said to Nadina.

"Zagreb is a wonderful city. It is very old and has much history, but it is also very modern. You Americans think that countries like Croatia are so different. Has it been that different so far? We know about America because we see so many films. But you know nothing about our country."

"Let me tell you something about those films," I said, a bit defensively. "Most of the people I've met have two images of America. The first is like *Boyz N the Hood*, with crime and drugs on every corner. The second is like *Beverly Hills 90210*. You think that everyone is either rich or on crack.

That's nowhere near the average person's life. That's why I hope you come to the United States so you can see for yourself."

"And your image of Croatia and Bosnia is so accurate, is it?" I could see from her reaction why these people are so passionate. "You think that we are so far behind you in everything. Your television cameras show pictures of peasants and old people. That is not an accurate picture at all. We are a very well educated country. Our culture is far richer and older than yours, and before independence Yugoslavia had one of the strongest armies in the world. You have no idea how similar we are to you conceited Americans."

She was right. Before I came to Croatia the only images I had were those shown to me on the six o'clock news. I had no knowledge of the richness and intelligence of this culture. I was also beginning to find myself very attracted to Nadina. She was strange and mysterious. I wondered if I should say anything or let her know how I felt. We would be together for several days so I decided to be patient and wait.

Suncokret had made arrangements for us to stay at a hostel on the outskirts of the city.

The hostel was primarily for travelers who were volunteering for various humanitarian organizations around Croatia. It was a way station of sorts, somewhere to stay until you got to where you were really going. After spending a full hour driving around Zagreb, we finally arrived. I had grown accustomed to not knowing quite where I was going or what was happening. Though most people around me spoke English, communication was still strained. They tried to be clear, but I was somehow always wondering what they meant.

The hostel was run by four people, including one American. He was the first American I had seen since arriving in Croatia except, of course, for the man in my dream. We were shown to the third floor, or sleeping floor. There was no privacy. It was a large room filled with at least twenty mattresses. Men and women shared the same quarters. Nadina and I found two mattresses near each other. Our three French friends were not pleased. They were older and did not expect such simple, open accommodations. I suppose they were expecting a hotel. Nadina made several snide remarks about the French. She was, in fact, quite irritated by their response. She said that this was quite common, people coming to help, being exposed to the hardships people endure here every day, then bitching. Many people in Bosnia didn't have homes, let alone beds.

That night we met a young man from England who was trying to find a way to get into Sarajevo. The three of us decided to walk to a pub down the road and have a beer. He had been offered a job teaching English, assuming, of course, he could get there. This, apparently, was the problem. There were two ways into Sarajevo, the first by air and the second by tunnel. With the Bosnian Serbs controlling the hills around the city, air travel was dangerous. The only other option was to walk several miles through a tunnel beneath the mountains that was barely high enough to stand in. This is how food and supplies had been smuggled in for years. The Serbs had a stranglehold on Sarajevo, and it was nearly impossible to enter or leave at that time.

We sat at a table outside the pub for several hours. A few others from the hostel joined us and before long we had a small crowd. The conversation switched back and forth between Croatian and English. I was apparently the only person at the table who didn't speak Croatian, so the shifting was for my benefit. It became clear that these people were much the same as any friends I had back in the States. In fact, aside from the language, this could have been nearly any bar in the United States. The music was the same, the beer, and of course, the laughter.

I went inside to buy Nadina a drink. Beside the bar was a table full of young Croatian women. They were obviously drunk and were making a scene. One of them grabbed my arm and said something I didn't understand.

"I'm sorry, but I don't speak Croatian."

Her eyes lit up. "Are you an American?" she asked.

"Yes."

"Oh, please sit down with us. We are all looking for an American to marry us and take us away from here," she said, laughing. "You can have your choice." She pulled out a stool and practically forced me into it.

"Why are you here in Croatia?" another woman asked.

"I'm a musician. I'm here to do a peace concert."

"Oh, a peace concert, that is something we need. What is your name?"

"My name is Jimmy."

As the others told me their names, the woman who spoke first took my hand and placed it on her leg. They were all very attractive but I wasn't interested in a quick fling, no matter what fantasy it might fulfill for them. Just then I saw Nadina walk into the bar. I gave her a look of desperation. She immediately walked to the table, said something to the women in Croatian, then took my hand and led me outside. I don't know what she said but the women were quite surprised.

"What do you think you are doing?" she asked me. "Surely you can see how badly they would all love to get their hooks into you. American men are not very common here anymore. Most Croatian women would love for you to marry them and bring them home."

"So why don't I marry you? Then your problem would be solved."

"Thanks but no thanks," she said, laughing. "I want to come to the United States, but not enough to have a fake marriage."

"I just thought we should examine every possibility."

"When I marry it will be for love, no other reason. So many women here would get married just so they could leave. I think marriage means much more than that."

"You never know," I said. "Sometimes things happen that we don't expect. Maybe you should keep your options open."

She smiled suspiciously. "What are you trying to say?"

"Nothing in particular. I just think you should keep an open mind. If there's one thing I've learned since I've been here, it's that you need to be prepared for whatever happens."

"I'll try to remember that," Nadina said. "Tomorrow we will go to the embassy and see what they say. But unlike you, I am not optimistic."

After another beer we went back to the hostel. The French people were already asleep. Nadina and I lay down near each other.

"Do you know anything about a secret spiritual community in Croatia that does some kind of healing work?" I asked her.

"They call themselves Emissaries of Light, or something?"

"No. Why?"

"I'm not sure," I said. "I had a strange dream about them and then Snjezana said something. I have a feeling that something incredible is going to happen."

"You mean you had a dream and you think it's going to come true?"

"More than that. There have been some unbelievable coincidences since I've been here. I really think that Gordana and Snjezana know more than they're telling me. And I have a strong feeling about all of it."

"Well, I don't believe in that kind of stuff, but if anything does happen you have to bring me. I need some excitement."

I promised and we both went to sleep.

The next day Nadina and I took a bus to the center of Zagreb. I was scheduled to appear on television at seven o'clock that evening, so Nadina decided to spend the day showing me around the city. Zagreb is a beautiful city, just as she said. In the very center is a huge open square and most streets radiate out from there. The city had been bombed twice, as recently as a month before I arrived. Apparently the Croatian Army had retaken a city that was held by the Bosnian Serbs, and in retaliation the Serbs dropped bombs over Zagreb. These bombs were designed to explode in midair, then drop small explosive devices with tiny parachutes onto the city below. The little bombs fall randomly and explode on impact with the power of several grenades. Nadina showed me a park near the square where a bomb had exploded, killing two people.

I had a one o'clock appointment at the American embassy. I had already called a woman there and said I was working on a major peace concert that would take place in Zagreb a year later. I thought that if they believed I needed Nadina to come back to the United States to help organize the concert, perhaps they would give her a visa. We stopped at a café around the corner from the American embassy to go over our plan. I would go alone. Perhaps they would be more willing to talk to an American citizen. Nadina would wait at the café. As we sat waiting, Nadina pointed out several ordinary-looking men in suits sitting on park benches, smoking cigarettes, or standing at bus stops. She said these men were undercover security guards watching for suspicious characters loitering around the embassy. Things were very tense and everyone was nervous.

I walked around the corner to the embassy. A guard at the door stopped me and asked me my business. I told him I had an appointment with the visa office. He told me to wait while he went inside to check. A moment later he came outside and invited me in. Another guard with a metal detector asked me to stop. He waved the wand around my body. Then the first guard asked me to take everything out of my pockets and leave it in a tray. I was given a claim ticket. After signing in, an automatic door opened and I walked into the main office.

I had never been inside an embassy. The visa office was unimpressive. There were a number of tables and a wall of bulletproof glass with small openings to speak through, behind which sat several officers. I was told to wait at the end. I had scheduled an appointment with the Deputy Director of the Visa Department. After a moment she appeared and sat down on the other side of the glass. She introduced herself.

I did my best to look professional. "I want

to get information on the procedure for bringing a Bosnian citizen to the United States to help organize a major event for peace here in Zagreb next spring."

"First of all, Mr. Twyman, securing a visa for a Bosnian citizen is a very complicated matter. The United States has already allowed its allotment of Bosnian refugees into the country, and that number can only be increased under very special circumstances."

She seemed like a nice woman so I tried a new approach—charm. "Yes, I understand that," I said. "That's why I came to you, because you seem like the kind of person who will understand my situation. You see, when I return to the United States I'm going to need someone with me to communicate with the committee members back here. I also think it would be very important to have someone with me who understands what's happening here. Essentially, I don't think we can pull this off without someone from Bosnia."

I thought my argument was a good one. It seemed like she was willing to help, but the more she explained the procedure, the more pessimistic I became. When the conversation was nearly finished she leaned forward and spoke a bit softer.

"Mr. Twyman, how much longer do you plan on staying in Croatia?"

"Probably no more than a week and a half," I told her.

She appeared concerned. I could tell by the look on her face that she wanted to tell me something. "I'm going to ask a guard to bring you around to my office. I need to speak with you privately."

A moment later a guard came into the sitting room and escorted me down a hall. He stopped in front of a door, opened it, and motioned for me to go inside. "Please sit down," the woman said. She sat behind a desk in a small but pleasant office. I sat in the chair in front of her. Behind her hung a picture of Bill Clinton, and a degree from Harvard Law School.

"It's no secret, Mr. Twyman, that situations are changing in this area of the world. I have the feeling that you aren't too aware of just how dangerous things are here. I called you into my office because I didn't want to say publicly what I'm about to tell you. For some time now Croatia has been marshaling its forces to begin an all-out offensive against the Bosnian Serbs in order to reclaim the land overtaken four years ago. We believe that this offensive will take place any time now. It's hard to tell what the consequences of that action will be, but you may want to consider leaving before it happens. I'm not trying to scare you, but we are asking all American citizens to be on alert. This is a very dangerous time and you can't be too careful."

"I'm not sure what you're saying," I told her. "Am I currently in danger here?"

"Once again, Mr. Twyman, we don't know what will happen. Prejudice runs very deep and it would be best not to be around when things explode. For the last four years the Croatian Army has been preparing for a major battle. Until now the Serbs have been able to take whatever they wanted, but when the offensive begins there will be no way of knowing what will happen. If the Croats are unable to defeat the Serbs it will be very bad here. Please, take my advice and leave as soon as you can."

I thanked her and went back to find Nadina.

* * *

Two days later I was scheduled to perform at a refugee camp on the outskirts of Zagreb. An organization called the Croatian League of Peace had organized all of my Zagreb appearances. Nadina decided to spend the day visiting friends and I was escorted around town by the director of the league, a woman named Naneda. Naneda was an interesting and outspoken woman who possessed the ability to organize and orchestrate events easily and effectively. The church concert was a great success and the television program had an unexpected surprise. I had been told that it was an interview program and that I was invited to be a guest. It turned out that I was *the* guest for the entire hour-and-a-half-long program. The host had studied in the United States and his English was flawless. He would ask a question and I would answer. When I finished, he gave a brief summary of my answer in Croatian. I kept my eye on the monitor in front of us. Whenever the camera turned away from me I frantically wiped my sweat-covered face. An hour and a half beneath hot studio lights left me dehydrated.

I met Naneda at her office and we left in her car for the refugee camp just outside Zagreb. It was built four years earlier when Muslim and Croatian refugees first came pouring into the city. When we pulled up to the front gate I was startled by the high wire fence and barrackslike buildings. It looked more like a concentration camp than a temporary residence for displaced victims of war. I immediately felt a heaviness in my chest. I could sense the hopelessness in the air, and I hadn't even walked through the gate.

I took my guitar out of the backseat and we went inside the camp. Two men leaning against the fence watched me suspiciously. To their left was a row of long white buildings, and to the right was a large yard filled with people. Most of the people were middle-aged or older. They sat on the grass in small groups. Many of the women were turning some sort of a wheel attached to a piece of wood. I asked Naneda what they were doing. She explained that these women spent the whole day grinding coffee for the rest of the camp. Others were knitting or sewing small pieces of cloth. I felt as if all their eyes were on us as we passed. I was nervous and asked Naneda where we were going.

"There is a community building at the other end of the camp," she explained. "This is where you will perform. A notice was posted there to let everyone know about the concert. It is hard to say how many will come. Often we plan events but the crowd is small. You see, when you live in this environment all the time without hope of leaving or your life changing in any way, you become discouraged. Even when there is something happening it is easy to sit in the yard and not participate. Also the children are almost always unattended. This is something else that is very common in this environment. The women are unable to take care of themselves or their family. They just sit and grind coffee."

We arrived at the far end of the property and came to a large, rickety aluminum building. This was the community center. We tried to go inside but the door was locked. Naneda told me to wait while she went to find someone to open it. I leaned my guitar against the building and sat down on a bench. The ground was strewn with garbage. Many of the buildings had graffiti painted on them, much like in the poor neighborhoods of many U.S. cities.

Several young boys were playing across the small road, and when they saw my guitar they came over. They spoke Croatian to me and seemed to want me to take the guitar out so they could play it. I smiled and said it had to stay inside the case. A few minutes later there were more children, and after a few minutes more there were at least one hundred children, some jumping in my lap, trying to take the guitar, and pulling on my leg. I tried to communicate as best I could but they didn't seem to understand me.

"They want to play your guitar," a ten-year-old blond-haired boy said to me.

"Can you explain to them that I can't take it out just yet," I screamed over the noise of the children.

"It does not matter, they will not listen to me either. My name is Vladimir." He held out his hand to me.

"I'm Jimmy. It's nice to meet you. How long have you lived here, Vladimir?"

"I have been here for four years. I am from Bosnia. Where are you from?"

"I guess both Boston and Chicago. It depends on who you ask."

"Why are you here?"

"I'm going to do a concert in the community center," I told him, happy to have someone to talk to.

"You will not be able to do your concert. The children will never be quiet long enough." He grabbed hold of a small girl, also with blond hair. "This is my sister. You can call her Sara because you cannot say her real name."

I reached down and touched her cheek. She grabbed hold of my hand and held onto it. Sara was beautiful. Her long blond hair ended past her shoulders in big curls, reminding me of Shirley Temple. I sat back down on the bench and set her on my lap.

"Where are you from?" I asked her, looking at Vladimir for the answer.

"We are all from Bosnia," he said. "I learned to speak English in school and from my mother."

Naneda walked up with a woman who opened the aluminum door. The children ran inside, screaming as they went. The noise bounced off the aluminum walls and echoed in my ears. The sound was unbearable. The woman tried to calm them down but it was impossible. I looked over at Vladimir, who stood near the corner of the room smiling at me. He was right, I would not be able to do a concert. No adults came to the building. I don't know if it was because of the noise or because they weren't interested. Through all of this Sara stood next to me, holding my hand.

Naneda finally came up to me. "I'm sorry for this," she said. "Maybe we should go."

I put my guitar back in the case and we walked outside. The children followed us, huddled so close to me that it was hard to walk. Sara helped keep some of the children away. One of her hands held mine and the other pushed away any of the children that got too close. When we finally got to the gate only Sara and Vladimir were left.

"Do you see?" Vladimir asked. "I told you that you would not be able to do a concert. These children are crazy."

I reached down and picked up Sara. "What do you say I bring the two of you back to America with me?"

"No, things will get better here, I am sure of it. Someday we will be able to go home again."

I sat Sara down and said goodbye. Naneda and I got into the car and we drove back to Zagreb. I didn't say a word the whole ride.

FOUR

The Guide

Jainist Prayer for Peace

Peace and Universal Love is the essence
of the Gospel preached by all the
Enlightened Ones.
The Lord has preached that equanimity
is the Dharma.
Forgive do I creatures all,
and let all creatures forgive me.
Unto all have I amity, and unto none enmity.
Know that violence is the root cause of
all miseries in the world.
Violence, in fact, is the knot of bondage.
"Do not injure any living being."

This is the eternal, perennial, and unalterable way of spiritual life.

A weapon, howsoever powerful it may be, can always be superseded by a superior one; but no weapon can, however, be superior to nonviolence and love.

—The Peace Seeds

My Croatian tour was nearly at an end. I had learned a great deal about the war and the people who were caught in it. Part of me was anxious to leave. There were so many hopeless, helpless victims of this drama. Day after day I met people who were waiting, I'm not sure for what. Some were waiting to go home. Others were waiting for revenge. I was waiting to do my workshop, then return to Italy.

I returned to Rijeka and began preparing for the workshop. I had given many such talks in the United States but had never taught in a non-English-speaking country.

Snjezana and Gordana would take turns interpreting. I would talk for about twenty seconds, then stop. Any more and they were afraid they would forget what I said. Most people spoke English but we decided on this approach for the few who didn't.

The workshop was set for Saturday, from one to five. It was to be held in the apartment owned by Suncokret in the center of town. Gordana had sent notices to all the meditation groups in the area, while Snjezana posted flyers around town. I was also asked to speak at two or three meditation classes. Judging from the response it seemed we would have a large group for the workshop.

I had been staying at Nadina's apartment for about two weeks. Living with a refugee family was a valuable learning experience. Each morning Nadina and Neda would go to Suncokret while Ned and I went to the playground to play basketball. Each day ten to twenty men would meet to play, while another even larger group gathered at the adjacent lot to play soccer. Several of the men were quite good. I felt about as inadequate and unskilled there as I did on any court. But

I loved to play, and they were excited to have an American, no matter how bad I was.

Each night we watched videos and cooked. I quickly learned of the generous nature of Bosnians. When you are a guest in their home, you are family. To refuse any hospitality is the greatest insult. If you are asked to stay you don't leave until your business is done. At one point I felt I had imposed on them long enough, a typical "guests are like fish" American attitude. When Nadina heard I was considering a vacant apartment on the Adriatic, she was hurt. She barely talked to me for two days. Finally she told me what was bothering her. She said that I obviously did not like staying with her family or I wouldn't want to leave. I explained that it had nothing to do with not liking her family, but that I didn't want to impose.

"That's fine for you," she said, "but when a Bosnian offers something, it comes from the heart. We don't make offers like this lightly." She explained that to leave is to reject not only the offer but the family as well. Nadina's offer for me to stay at her apartment was a greater honor than I knew. I politely refused the other apartment and stayed there.

Nadina had decided not to come to the workshop. Though she was interested in spirituality, she didn't feel ready. She and Snjezana had grown very close, an influence that was very positive for Nadina. I was sorry she wasn't coming. I was very attracted to her, especially since our trip to Zagreb. It amazed me that I was developing such close relationships in Croatia. My three friends, Nadina, Snjezana, and Gordana, had already become an important part of my life.

Gordana had cleaned and nicely arranged the room for the workshop. I spent Saturday morning alone, praying and organizing my thoughts. When I arrived at the apartment the room was full. Nearly thirty people were there. Some were familiar with the Course, and others were not but were interested anyway. Burning incense filled the room with the scent of sandalwood. Candles were appropriately arranged, giving the space a mystical glow and radiance. I stood in the doorway for a moment, looking in. Of the thirty or so people, there was one man. I was used to female-dominated groups, but in Croatia spirituality and meditation were especially women's affairs, not meant for rough and macho men. After a moment everyone turned around and saw me.

"And here is our dear brother Jimmy," Gordana said.

I was thrilled by the warmth and openness these people showed me. I sat down on a pillow facing them.

"Thank you, everyone, for inviting me to give this talk. I can't tell you how excited I am, not only to find so much love and peace here, but to find so many people interested in *A Course in Miracles*. The *Course* is meant to bring you to a full experience of the truth within you. It teaches the path of forgiveness, or in other words, seeing what is real. The goal is to use the practice of forgiveness to experience what has always been true: that you are still as God created you. As the *Course* says, if you remain as God created you, then sin, guilt, sickness, and death are not real, but are illusions you have made up in your mind to avoid the truth. Forgiveness helps us look past these illusions to what is real. Once we have done this we can live in a loving experience that the world doesn't understand. It is a joy that exists alone, beyond time and space, in the unbounded reaches of eternity. This is your home—pure joy. *A Course in Miracles* is nothing more than a tool to show you that you have never left that home."

As I was saying these words, a tall, black-haired man stepped into the room and sat down in the back. He had piercing dark eyes that seemed to look right through me. I found myself concentrating my energy and attention on him. As my eyes would scan the room they always rested back on him. He projected a peaceful, loving energy that made me feel at ease. His smile was warm and real.

After a bit more than an hour of talking I decided it was time for a break. Everyone began to leave the room and Gordana took me by the hand.

"That was wonderful, my darling. Now I have a friend I am very anxious for you to meet."

The black-haired man stood up to greet me. I felt as if I fell into his eyes, they were so deep and vast. "My name is Duro," he said. "I am very happy to meet you, Jimmy."

"This is the man you were telling me

about," I said to Snjezana. I turned back to Duro. "I am very happy to finally meet you as well," I said. "I feel as though you have been the greatest mystery of my stay in Croatia. I have heard of you and yet I know nothing about you."

"We will have plenty of time to learn from each other," he said in a way I cannot explain. "You are a wonderful teacher. It is clear that you understand deeply all these things you talk about."

"Thank you," I said. "Will you be staying after the workshop?"

"Duro, Snjezana, and I will take you out to dinner after the workshop," Gordana said. "We will have plenty of time to talk then."

"Wonderful," I said. Just then a woman squeezed next to Snjezana.

"Jimmy, I am getting so much out of your talk," she said. I smiled at Duro to let him know I looked forward to spending more time with him. Then I turned toward the woman.

The workshop ended shortly after five. When everyone had left, Gordana, Snjezana, Duro, and I locked up and decided on a restaurant. There was a nice outdoor café directly across the street. After we were seated and had ordered coffee, Gordana began:

"Jimmy, it is time for us to explain a few things to you. Please do not think that Snjezana and I have deceived you, because as we have said, we know very little. When I first received your letter of introduction I had a very strange feeling. There was something about the things you said that stirred me. I brought the letter to Duro. He is my teacher. I knew that he would know if there was something important about what I was feeling. Without hesitating he said that you must come. I asked him why but he wouldn't tell me. All he said was that you must come to Croatia. This is why I invited you. And this is all I know."

I turned to Duro. "Why was it important for me to come here, Duro?"

He looked at me and smiled. "I will begin at the beginning," he said. "All through history humanity has been in conflict. This conflict reveals itself in every relationship, including between large groups of people. When this feeling of conflict becomes great, nations go to war. The fighting kills thousands, or millions. As you said in your workshop, conflict in the world is the result of the feeling of conflict within us. We project that feeling into the world because we are not ready to accept that we are the cause, and therefore the solution, to that conflict. Thus wars have raged in the world since the beginning of time, because we were not ready to deal with the conflict where it really is, within us.

"For thousands of years there has been a secret society whose responsibility it was to give humanity the chance to mature. This society has always existed near a place in the world where the conflict is greatest, in a country or area experiencing the most hatred, greed, and war. This is because the power of their work is greatest when it dissolves conflict from the center, or from the place where it is thickest. These people therefore live silently, invisibly, without ever being noticed, in the center of despair, in the middle of conflict. Their work is not seen by the world. It is a spiritual work, its function being to extend the magnificence of Divine Light through all the world. In this way they inspire peace, they give hope and instill the desire for forgiveness. Wars end, people and nations learn from their mistakes. Each time, humanity comes a little closer to accepting the truth of creation, that peace and conflict both reside within, and it is only there that it can be resolved, experienced, and lived. This community, called the Emissaries of Light, will continue to exist in areas of extreme conflict until this has happened. Then it will not be needed.

"And that day is coming soon," he said. "It is when the world seems the farthest away from peace that it is closest. If you look at the world it is clear that we have more power, more weaponry, and more hate than ever before. But at the same time, there is more understanding, more hope, and more desire for peace than the world has ever known. These two seemingly opposite experiences indicate that humanity is growing close to the time appointed for it to move past its separate-mind, warring-thought system, to a world of peace, cooperation, and harmony. This has been indicated by the global changes observed in recent years. It has also been prophesied by all the ancient cultures and religions. This is the time they were all referring to. But none of them were aware of the work and mission of the Emissaries. This is because it was essential that their presence and influence remain a secret. Their function has been to remain hidden, doing their work for humanity and silently setting the stage for the day when their job would not be required. This would happen when humanity had matured to accept responsibility for what it has created. That time is nearly here."

"You said that these Emissaries of Light have been around for thousands of years," I said. "How have they been able to remain hidden, and how do they continue when each generation dies?"

"How they have remained hidden is impossible to say," Duro said. "Emissaries possess a divine understanding that is unknown to the rest of us. They are able to be, or not be, wherever they choose. As far as continuing after they die, when each Emissary has finished their work they are released. This does not mean that they die, but are somehow changed. You might call this ascension. When this happens they need to be replaced because a particular number must be maintained. One is called to be an Emissary. I am not sure how this happens. One who has been chosen simply finds themselves there, without explanation.

Perhaps they feel an uncontrollable urge to visit a part of the world they have never been to, perhaps a place that is involved in a terrible war. No one understands why they go, but they do. Once there they are led to the community, which is always hidden away in some remote area. When they arrive they realize that this is the place they were searching for. Then they assume their place around the wheel."

This made me very nervous. He had just described what happened to me. I had a mysterious desire to come to Bosnia and Croatia, against the advice of everyone I knew. They thought I was crazy, but I had to go. Was it possible that what he was saying was true, and that I had been "chosen"? This thought terrified me. I felt like standing up, walking to the bus station, and getting out.

Gordana and Snjezana sat very still without saying a word. It was obvious that they were hearing this story for the first time as well. I thought about the dream I had nearly two weeks before. It seemed consistent with what Duro was saying. I remembered the wheel and the man I was so completely drawn to. And I remembered what he said to me about peace and the world. Was there a connection between these two? I told Duro about my dream. He listened intently, then paused.

"That is very interesting," he finally said. "You already know more than I expected. Many things you described in your dream are accurate. Let me tell you more about myself and perhaps you will understand.

"I am a doctor. Several years ago, before the war, I was hiking in a remote part of Croatia searching for medicinal herbs and plants I use in my practice. I was alone. At one point during my journey I became very dizzy. I felt I would faint. I must have blacked out because the next thing I knew I was lying in a small hut. I was alone except for an old woman, who sat in a chair in the corner. She watched me but did not say a word. I sat up and looked around. There were no furnishings, just the mat I woke up on, and the chair. I looked out the window and saw several other small huts roughly the same size as the one I was in. I walked out the door. It seemed as if there was no one else around. On the other side of the huts in front of me was a large round building. I began to walk in its direction. When I got closer I realized it wasn't round at all, but that it had twelve sides. Just then I saw a young man come out of a small wooden door. He saw me and motioned for me to come inside with him.

"When I stepped inside I had a feeling of light-headedness, almost like the way I felt when I was on my hike. The huge room was very bright, and yet there were no windows. My eyes actually had to adjust to the brightness. When they did I was able to look around and see everything. The building was very large with a design on the floor, just like you described from your dream. Around the circle, at twelve points indicated by the design, sat twelve people. In the very center sat a man. There was a light haze above them, like a cloud of smoke. I also noticed that to one side stood five young men, similar in age to the one who was standing with me. I later learned that these men were attendants. Their job was to provide for the needs of the twelve people around the wheel, six men and six women.

"After a few moments the young man took me back outside. That was the first time I ever visited the Emissaries of Light. Like the others, I was called there, but not to be part of the wheel. My role is more removed, like a liaison. I go back when I am called. My role is to be the link between here and there. In order for them to do their work I need to attend to certain things in the world. And that is how I found you. You have not been called to be an Emissary. Like me, you have been chosen for a very particular function. Since the very beginning there has always been someone like me to act somewhere between the wheel and the world. There has never been anyone like you. Your function is unlike anything that has ever happened before. The reason is because of what we were talking about earlier, the changes taking place in the world. Until now the work of the Emissaries has remained a secret. It must now be made public. Everyone must know of their work, and of their own readiness to step into a global experience of peace and harmony. Your role is to learn the practice and the spirituality of the Emissaries, then make it available to everyone in the world."

I was still frightened, but part of me wanted to laugh out loud. Another part understood what he was saying. "Even if everything you've said is true, why me?

What's so special about me to get such a job?"

"Nothing," he said. "There's nothing special about you. Perhaps that's why. This is not about being special, but having what is needed to do the job. I have no idea why you were chosen, only that you were. None of us know why we are asked to do certain things. It has to do with our gifts. You are a great teacher. Perhaps that's why. I'm also told you are a writer. That may help as well. Ultimately, the reasons are beyond us, but they are choices that we have made ourselves. You are here because you chose to be here. And you will fulfill whatever function you have because you choose to. Nothing will happen without your consent or permission. You will find out why you were chosen, starting tomorrow."

"What do you mean?" I asked.

"Tomorrow I'm taking you to the Emissaries, and Gordana and Snjezana as well. You are all involved in this. You all have a role to play."

"Wait a minute," I said. "I'm leaving Croatia in two days. I have concerts still planned in Italy."

"Why don't you bring your guitar with

you?" Snjezana said. "Maybe the Emissaries would like a concert."

"Hold on," I said, irritated by such assumptions. "I'm not trying to doubt this or anything, but the whole story is a little hard to believe. You want me to drop all my plans and march off to God-knows-where in the middle of a war zone to find some mythical community I'm not even sure exists. It's not that I don't trust you, but I'd have to be out of my mind to even consider such a thing."

Gordana leaned forward and touched my hand. "Jimmy, you know that we would never do anything to hurt you. I trust Duro. Whatever he says I believe. I agree, it does sound fantastic, but look at everything that has happened to you so far. Everything has led to this. I'm sure that if you look inside yourself you will feel that this is real, and that you must do this."

She was right. I did feel it. As frightened as I was, I knew that everything Duro said was true. They were asking me to release every ounce of common sense I had left and go off into the mountains of Croatia searching for a building with twelve sides and thirteen people sitting around a wheel saving the world. I had to block the voice that was trying to keep me away. I had come this far and I wasn't about to turn back now.

"We will leave in the morning," Duro said. "You will bring only clothes, nothing else. It is very important that you leave behind any electronic devices or cameras. We will drive in my car as far as we can, then we will walk the rest. If we are lucky we will arrive by night."

"There's one more thing," I said.

"What is it, Jimmy?" Gordana asked.

"Nadina has to come."

"No one else may come," Duro said.

"Then I'm not going. I made Nadina a promise and I intend to keep it. If she can't come then you can forget about me."

Duro looked over at Gordana. She nodded her head.

"All right then," he said. "Until morning."

FIVE

The Secret

Jewish Prayer for Peace

Come, let us go up to the mountain of
the Lord, that we may walk the
paths of the Most High.
And we shall beat our swords into plough-
shares, and our spears into pruning
hooks.
Nation shall not lift up sword against nation—
neither shall they learn war any more.
And none shall be afraid, for the mouth of
the Lord of Hosts has spoken.

—THE PEACE SEEDS

Nadina and I were waiting outside her apartment at six-thirty the following morning. Duro had said to only bring clothes. I hoped he wouldn't mind that I had brought my toothbrush. I wasn't sure how closely I should follow his orders. Aside from that, Nadina and I were in full accord.

Duro pulled up in a small station wagon moments later. Snjezana and Gordana were with him. We threw our things in the back and got in. Before long we were on the highway heading out of Rijeka. I had no idea where we were going, but this seemed to be part of the plan. The location of the Emissary community was a closely guarded secret. Even if he had told me where it was, it wouldn't have mattered. Aside from the road between Rijeka and Zagreb, I was lost. Duro had mentioned that we were heading toward the border of Bosnia. I was told that this was the area held by the Serbs.

"That is correct," Duro said. "That is why this is very dangerous. We will be very near two towns that are held by the Serbs. But you shouldn't worry. We will park the car in an area that is very safe, then we will hike through the hills to the community. I have done this many times without incident. I know how to slip between the Serbs."

This was like telling a deer not to worry on the first day of hunting season. I was apparently the only one who was concerned by this. Perhaps they were numb from the constant threat of war, but the thought of slipping into an area held by the Serbs was not my idea of fun. It took every ounce of trust I had to put my faith in Duro. He was confident and serene, as if we were out for a drive in the country.

I had told Nadina about our dinner conversation when I arrived back at her house the night before. At first she thought I was making it up. When she realized I was serious she became very excited, especially when she heard that she could come along. I had had a hard time sleeping that night. When I did, my dreams were violent. Images of battles and bombs haunted me all night long. I began to question my decision to go along on this crazy journey. I should be on my way back to Assisi, but instead I was heading right into the heart of the battlefield. It was too late to retreat.

We drove for nearly five hours, stopping only once to get gas. We had left the highway long ago. We drove along narrow and sometimes nonexistent roads. I saw an occasional burned-out car at the side of the road. This was apparently an area once held by the Serbs. The countryside was beautiful. The contrast of the rolling green hills made where we were going seem surreal. I had to remind myself that we were in a serious situation. This was not just an ordinary tour through a foreign country. They were at war, and that was something I had never seen. I didn't know how people live during a war. I had assumed they did their best to stay away from it, but here we were driving right into it.

Duro pulled into the drive of what appeared to be an abandoned farmhouse. He drove to the back and parked the car behind a barn. "This is where we start walking," he said. "We must hurry or we will not make it before the sun goes down. It will take nearly six hours to hike from here."

We took our belongings from the back and Duro led us through a field till we finally came to a narrow dirt road. We walked silently for a very long time. Duro led the way, followed by Gordana, then me. Snjezana and Nadina were arm-in-arm several yards behind me. The forest was alive with the sounds of birds singing and squirrels playing. The sun streamed through the trees, casting moving shadows across the forest floor. After a long while I walked ahead to Duro.

"Duro, tell me about the man who sits in the middle of the wheel. What is his role?"

"The twelve Emissaries sit around the wheel, each one in their own place. They represent all life on the planet, much like the zodiac with its twelve signs. Their job is to focus a particular color light ray through the symbols of the diagram to the center. The color of light they focus indicates the level or part of humanity they represent. As each Emissary extends the light and focuses it to the center of the wheel, the One in the Center takes each of those rays and gathers them together, then projects the Divine Light to the whole universe. He is the hub of the wheel and the Emissaries are the spokes. The light that the One in the Center projects is pure, healing energy. Imagine a huge fountain in the center of a great plain. The fountain sends an enormous stream of water into the air that spreads in every direction. Then it falls across the whole plain, encouraging growth and keeping it from being desolate and dead. This is very similar to the work of the Emissaries."

"Who is the One in the Center?" I asked.

"That is very difficult to explain," he said. "The One in the Center has no identity as you and I would understand. You could say that he is all identity since his role is to focus the attention of humanity into one healing stream of energy. Each Emissary has a name, just like you and me, and after their twelve-hour meditation they will sometimes talk to the attendants and seem very normal. The One in the Center never does this. He rarely talks with anyone else in the community. When the meditation is over he returns to his hut until the next day. I have never had a conversation with him. His role is so specific and important that he doesn't relate to the world of form at all."

"You said that the Emissaries have existed for thousands of years, but that they are always located in a place where there is tremendous hatred and violence. That doesn't make sense. Do they get up and move every few years whenever one war ends and another war begins?"

"The easiest way to understand is to say that they have existed in one form or another for thousands of years. As times change, so do the Emissaries. But the one thing that has never changed is the wheel. The symbols that comprise the wheel are the binding force that defines the Emissaries' role and keeps them active, age after age. After a period of time, or when a particular place in the world no longer experiences the hatred and violence that formed the wheel, the circle reappears somewhere else—perhaps with the same people, perhaps not. This continuous cycle leads ultimately to the time when the wheel is no longer needed. This time is very near. When a sufficient number of people begin extending Divine Light themselves, then the Emissaries will cease to exist."

"What will we do when we get to the community?" I asked him.

"I do not know. My role is to bring you there, that is all. I do not even know how long we will stay, perhaps a few days, perhaps more. I do know that everything will happen as it should. You can count on that."

We walked the entire afternoon. Duro seemed to know where he was going, though I could not find a path or a reason for the route he followed. I was beginning to get tired. Snjezana and Nadina started to complain. Though Gordana said nothing, I could tell she was tired as well. The sun was beginning to touch the horizon. It would be dark soon. I watched Duro to see if he was concerned. He was serene. I hoped we were getting close but there was no way to know. Then suddenly, Duro stopped.

We entered a long, narrow field. It was empty except for a scattering of trees and bushes. Duro led us straight up the middle. He seemed to be walking cautiously. I looked around but could see no reason for this. Then he stopped.

"Hold very still," he said in a whisper. No one moved. We stood like statues for more than a minute. Then he smiled and motioned for us to continue. I looked ahead and saw a small house no more than two hundred feet away. I didn't understand why I had not seen it before. In fact, it was nearly impossible not to see it. It rested on the edge of the field, a brown wooden structure that was completely obvious from any angle. I turned and looked at Snjezana, who also was surprised. A very tall woman then stepped out from behind the house and came to greet us. Duro walked ahead of us, and when he reached the woman he gave her a brief hug. Then he turned back to us. He spoke to her in Croatian. It seemed as if he were telling her about me.

"She doesn't speak English," he said to me. "Her name is Sonja. She lives in the community, cooking and doing other things. Everyone here has a task to fulfill, something that helps. She welcomes all of you."

Snjezana said something to her in Croatian, then Sonja asked us to leave our things beside the house. Then she led us past the house to a path that led through the forest. As I looked into the forest I could see small huts scattered about. After a minute or so we came to another one-story house, the same size as the first one we saw. We walked to the front door and went inside.

Several men sat at a table, two more in chairs next to a fire. When they saw us they all stood up and walked over to Duro. He hugged each one, then introduced us. When he introduced Nadina, Snjezana, and Gordana he spoke in Croatian. Then he turned to me.

"Jimmy, these men are the attendants I told you about. They live here in this house. Their role is to provide for the needs of the Emissaries."

I walked over and shook each one's hand. They seemed very friendly and happy we had come. Only two spoke English, Ivan and Toni. They all wore T-shirts and pants and were under forty.

"We have been waiting for you," Toni said. "One of the Emissaries told us you were coming. We will try to make all of you comfortable."

They pulled some extra chairs over to the table and we sat down. A pot of soup was simmering on a woodstove in the corner of the kitchen. Two of the men filled five bowls and brought them to where we were sitting. I had not realized how hungry I was. It was delicious. Duro was having an energetic conversation with the men as he ate. The whole scene seemed strange to me, as if this wasn't what I expected. It was so normal, not at all like the quiet, somber community I had expected.

"You will find that we are very normal indeed," Toni said.

"How did you know what I was thinking?" I asked him.

"You will also find that there are no private thoughts here. We are attendants because the Emissaries don't need to talk to us. They think what they need and we get it. It is very common here, you will get used to it."

"How long have you been an attendant?" I asked.

"For five years. I am from Split. One day a friend of mine asked me to come to a meditation class. I had never been before, so I agreed. During the class I felt as if I was in the mind of the leader. I could hear her thoughts as if they were my own. And I knew she was aware of this. After the meeting she said she must talk to me. She said she knew of a place where I could use this skill, but it meant a great sacrifice. I immediately knew that I must go to that place, even though I didn't know where or what it was. A week later I was here, and I have been here ever since."

"Do you know why I am here?"

"Of course," he said in a way that made it seem commonplace. "You are here to learn of Divine Light, then teach others how to extend it. They have been waiting for you a very long time. They have been waiting for the world to be ready for this. Now that it is, you will teach people about the Emissaries, and they will learn to do what Emissaries do. Then this place will be gone, and I can go back to Split."

He laughed and patted me on the shoulder. I immediately liked Toni. He was warm and gentle, but had an inner strength I felt instantly drawn to. He told me about the other attendants, how they found the community and where they were from. Most were from the Balkan region, two from Croatia, one from Bosnia, one from Serbia, and one from Albania. The sixth was from Austria. They were all happy and hospitable. We had visited with them for about an hour when Duro said it was time for us to get ready to retire. Sonja helped us find our way back to the house we saw when we first arrived. This is where we would stay. I learned that this house was normally for the five or six women who lived there. They had moved to the other side of the property while we were there.

The huts in the woods belonged to the twelve Emissaries. They lived solitary lives, extending the Divine Light for twelve hours each day, from midnight to noon, and spending the rest of their time alone in their hut or speaking with one of the attendants. They rarely came to the houses or visited with more than one person at a time. Their role was to hold the Light, and when they weren't meditating they were preparing for the next session.

When we arrived at the house we each found a bed and prepared for the night. In a few hours the rest of the community would begin the twelve-hour vigil. Duro felt it would be better if we got some rest and joined them in the morning. It had been a long day and we were exhausted. Duro and I shared a room. After a short time we went to bed.

"What's going to happen tomorrow?" I asked Duro.

"We'll join the last few hours of the meditation. I don't know what will happen after that. I'm sure they have already made plans but I don't know what they are."

"I have to admit, I'm very nervous. Part of me still doubts this is happening. I don't understand why they would choose me—I mean, maybe after they get to know me . . ."

"You weren't chosen for any of the reasons you think," Duro said. "It wasn't because you are the best at something or because you'll be able to teach this better than anyone else. You were chosen because it is already in you. This is not something you'll learn, it's something you'll remember. That's true for all of us. Extending the Divine Light is something we already do because everyone in the world is what the Divine Light is. But if we forget what we are, then our extension of the Light becomes muddled and unclear. This is a process of unlearning all the thoughts that block your extension of the Light, then everything you do will be a reflection of truth."

I rolled over and faced the wall. Though it was happening so fast, I somehow felt ready. I just wasn't sure what it was I was ready for. The dream I had about the wheel and the One who sat in the Center ran through my mind. Was he real? What would happen in the morning when I entered the circle for the first time? My journey to Croatia and Bosnia had brought far more than I ever expected. And the suspense about what would happen that next morning was enormous.

It was nearly nine o'clock when I woke up. The others were already up and dressed. A bowl of fruit sat on the kitchen table. Nadina sat in a chair eating an orange. She looked more alive than I had ever seen her. I was used to her being less than enthusiastic in the morning, her poor attitude second only to my own. But now she was radiant, as if she were breathing for the first time in her life.

"Good morning, Jimmy," she said as she stood up from her chair and gave me a hug. "I am so happy I am here, and I don't even know why. It is so beautiful and the people are so wonderful. Do you realize that I have not had a desire to smoke since I arrived? And neither has Snjezana. It is as if I never smoked at all."

Duro walked in the front door with Gordana. "You must eat quickly so we can attend the last few hours of the meditation session, Jimmy," Duro said.

I grabbed an apple and said I could eat it on the way.

"I'm afraid you can't do that," he said. "Last night was not too serious but we must still realize where we are. This is a very sacred spot, perhaps the most sacred place in all the world. Everything must be done with this sacredness in mind. For example, you don't eat when you walk. When you walk along these paths it must be done in complete reverence. Do only one thing at a time. I will explain more as we go. Go ahead and eat, then we will go."

When I finished the apple I walked outside. The others were waiting.

"We will walk to the circle in complete silence," Duro said. "When we arrive one of the attendants will show us where to sit. We will stay there until the meditation is over. Meditate however you choose. Don't worry about following any particular form. You will notice that the Emissaries do not move during meditation. Once you have been seated you will not move either. It is important that we cause as little disruption as possible."

We walked along the path in total silence.

I tried to keep my mind clear and open. We walked past the house we had eaten in the night before. Beyond the house was a small clearing, then another path. We followed that path another five minutes or so. I saw more huts in the woods. They were nestled in the forest as if they were protected and invisible if one weren't actually looking for them. The community blended in with the forest. It felt as if this place were part of the natural environment. Nothing obscured the balance and beauty of the area.

When we came to the end of the path Duro stopped. I looked in front of us and saw the meditation building. It was just as Duro had described it, though much taller than I had imagined, forty to fifty feet high. We walked to a small door where one of the attendants was waiting. He held the door open as each of us entered. We stood just inside until he came in. He led us around the outer wall only about thirty feet, then motioned for us to sit at least ten feet apart.

The first thing I noticed was the intensity of light, just as Duro had described. And yet it was not the same as walking into an extremely bright room, it was more like a brilliance that began somewhere within, then radiated outward. It is impossible to describe. The huge wheel with the ancient symbols took up nearly the entire floor. It was exactly as it was in my dream. Twelve people sat just inside the rim of the wheel, six men and six women, each enclosed within the spokes. They sat with their legs crossed, deep in meditation. The six attendants stood at various points against the outer wall. I came to learn that their function during the meditation was not to attend to the Emissaries physically, but to support them psychically. There was some kind of energy exchange that took place when an Emissary's mind wandered or began losing energy. The exchange revitalized the Emissary, helping to focus his or her mind.

I felt myself falling into a deep meditative state without effort. It was as if the environment was so supportive of peace and tranquillity that my mind responded immediately. My eyes remained half open. My gaze moved easily about the room. At the very top of the vaulted roof was a large skylight, at least seven feet square. The smoke from the incense hung like a cloud in the light. The room was nearly empty, except for tall candles burning in various places. There was no furniture at all. Everyone stood or sat on the floor. Then through a light cloud of smoke I saw the One in the Center. He was staring right at me, smiling. His eyes felt like a laser beam cutting through my mind. I turned away just for an instant. When I looked again his eyes were closed, the smile gone.

There was no question about it, he was the same man I saw in my dream. Though it was hard to see him clearly through the incense and bright light, I was sure it was him. My mind was falling into a deep, restful space. I felt as if I were one with the room, one with the people in the room. Thought was gone. My mind was quiet and still. I had never experienced such overwhelming peace before. The energy moved around and within me. The spaces and boundaries seemed to melt and merge with my experience, which could no longer be identified as bodily, but whole, complete, and unified.

I was unaware of the passing of time. I don't know how long I was in this state, perhaps ten minutes, perhaps two hours. My mind was like an immense body of water holding its breath. The water barely stirred, no waves or even the slightest ripple, just the gentle and silent beating of an unseen heart that lifted the water as if by a string, setting it down to rest to become the essence of clarity. And then in this silence I heard a voice. At first it was like a whisper beyond my reach, but then it grew louder and clearer. I was barely able to make out the words. "Seek not peace here, but find it everywhere. Seek not peace here, but find it everywhere." Each time I heard it, it grew louder and clearer. Over and over the voice came till I felt like it was all around me.

I opened my eyes and saw all twelve Emissaries and the One in the Center looking right at me. The voice was them. It was like a silent mantra that one started, joined each time by another, then another, mentally projecting the words across space. It startled me. I had never experienced such clarity and the certainty of shared thought. The One in the Center was smiling again, but this time much more than before. I felt as if I were jolted awake. A moment later the Emissaries turned their eyes to the center of the circle and began quietly chanting. I did not understand the language they were speaking. It didn't sound like anything I even recognized. After a few moments the chanting ended and they stood up and walked out the door, single file. The One in the Center was last, his eyes looking down when he passed me. We stood up as well and waited for everyone else to leave. When they had, Duro led us out the door. It was a bright, sunny day.

SIX

The One in the Center

Shinto Prayer for Peace

Although the people living
across the ocean
surrounding us, I believe,
are all our brothers and sisters,
why are there constant troubles in
this world?
Why do winds and waves rise in the
ocean surrounding us?
I only earnestly wish that the wind will
soon puff away all the clouds which are
hanging over the tops of the mountains.
—The Peace Seeds

I spent most of that first day alone. Something very profound had happened to me earlier that morning. I wasn't sure what it was, but it sent me flying in a space that was both unfamiliar and marvelous. I was incapable of holding a concrete thought. Everything drifted away as if there were nothing left for them to cling to. My mind was open, clear, and free. It was a strange feeling. I could almost sense my rational mind calling to me, as if it were removed and far away. Even with all my study of *A Course in Miracles*, I was suspicious of this new clarity. And yet the sense of peace was far too overwhelming to be dissipated by such fears. I felt as if my head had been opened like a can of sardines that had just been peeled back. I could feel the energy streaming from the top of my head. My senses were keen and alert. The sounds and sights of the forest came to life. I felt as if I were one with life, one with the universe.

"I see you have found me."

The voice came from somewhere to the left but I couldn't see anyone through the thick forest. I had been wandering for a long time and wasn't sure where I was. I stood still and waited.

"I said, I see you found me."

I looked again and saw the One in the Center standing thirty or so feet away from me. His pale green shirt and pants made him blend in easily with the trees and plants.

"I didn't know I was looking for you," I said.

"Of course you were. I was calling you. You may not have heard me with your ears, but your mind knew where to go. How are you feeling?"

I began walking in his direction. "I feel incredible," I said. "But also a little afraid. I've never experienced anything quite like this before."

"You will adjust," he said. "Your body needs time to adjust to the intensity of the Light here. It's like going from a dark room into one filled with light. In a few days it will even out and you will feel fine."

Just as in my dream, he was clearly an American. His voice was deep and strong. He was of average height, stout, with striking dark features. It was hard to tell his age. He could have been in his fifties, but I suspected he was older. His presence was riveting. I felt like a moth being drawn to the flame. There was something about him that my mind could not fathom, but that drew me close.

"I'm hoping you can answer a few questions," I said to him.

"Hold your questions for now. We do not have much time to accomplish all that we must. Do you know why you are here?"

I told him what I knew. He listened intently, not so much to my words but, it seemed, to every inflection, every movement, as if he was deciding something about me. When I finished, he smiled and asked me to walk with him. After a few minutes we came to a small hut. This was apparently his home. There was a fire pit filled with ashes and burning coals about fifteen feet from the front door. A few garden tools rested against the side of the hut and a shirt was drying on a line hung between two trees. As he took a few small pieces of wood from a pile and laid them on the coals, he motioned for me to sit down on a log. His movements were smooth and agile. He knelt over the wood until it caught fire. Then he sat down on a log across from me.

"You are here because your consciousness is about to become aware of itself. It's that simple. When you know yourself, you know the truth. When you refuse to know yourself, panic sets in as you seek a substitute, terror pursues you when you realize you can never replace the eternal, and fear seizes you when you experience guilt for trying. The idea that we are separate and alone is just that—an idea, a thought. It is not true. The truth in you has fallen asleep and is having a dream of separation. But the dream is almost over. Reality is about to give birth to reality, and that is why you are here, to help reality through the birth canal."

"How am I to do such a thing?" I asked him.

"Oh, it's already been done, that's the beauty of it. Sounds like a paradox, doesn't it? Actually, it's not. You see, a dreaming mind can create whatever world it wants, but it can't make it real. It can create entire worlds that run by completely different laws, but when that mind wakes up it finds that reality has never changed. Everything is the same as it was before the dream. And so it is with this physical world. When it's time for the alarm clock to go off, then that's what it does. You wake up, brush your teeth, and go about your day, never once considering that the dream was real. The alarm clock is about to go off, Jimmy. The awakening of humanity to its Divine Nature is almost here. Your job is to help make it easy, to make it smooth. Do you understand?"

"In theory, yes. But I'm not sure if I really do," I said. "I understand what you're saying, but I don't know how it applies to me. What am I going to do to bring about this awakening?"

"Whatever you have to do, I guess," he said, laughing. "Don't concern yourself with those questions, Jimmy. Your only job for now is to learn about the Emissaries. By learning about our work you'll know exactly what to do. All I can tell you is that people live in fear. As this awakening occurs that fear will have to be released. If it is not, then the birth will be traumatic. If fear is released and people are able to relax into these changes, the birth will be smooth and easy. Your job, then, is to help people release their fear. You'll do that by teaching them about peace."

"Is that why I'm here, because I teach peace already?"

"You're here because you chose this job," he said as he poked a stick at the coals, stirring the fire. "You signed up for this tour. Don't think that any of this is happening to you. To the contrary, it's happening by you. Your job is to communicate the experience of peace by teaching truth. What is the truth? Simply this: Humanity has chosen its own isolation, imposed its own exile. The pain, suffering, and loneliness of the world is born from the idea that humanity can be separate from God, or creation, or however you want to express the Divine. But once again, this is an idea, an attempt to make possible what is impossible. This is why it will inevitably fail.

"Humanity made an unfortunate 'Declaration of Independence.' In doing so it seemed to isolate itself from its source, an illusion that has brought suffering, pain, and death. But humanity has forgotten that it chose this isolation freely. Because it has the power of free will, it has the ability to experience anything it wishes. But it can't make the impossible real, and separation from source is impossible. It can only make it *seem* real. The awakening we speak of is really a 'Declaration of Dependence.' It is the willingness to accept the role of being a co-creator with God. By becoming completely dependent we experience power, a belief totally foreign to the ego, which believes the opposite. By declaring your dependence on God you release the illusion of separation and reassume your place in the Divine drama."

"How will I communicate this?" I asked him.

"By learning to work with Divine Light, or the essence of creation, you'll learn to communicate truth on every level. Your music will communicate an experience of peace that transcends the music and words. Your teaching will communicate a certainty that will be undeniable. And your writing will communicate the fundamentals of Light, or the intellectual understanding that will enable people to release their fear to experience truth. You will teach what you learn. You will give only that which you allow yourself to receive. This, in fact, is how teaching works."

He stood up and moved to a log just to my left. I could smell a deep, rich odor around him, as if he was the earth itself. His presence was riveting. He leaned forward and held my arm.

"For thousands of years the Emissaries of Light have prepared the world for this time. Our only function has been to keep the doors of heaven open, or to keep the flow of Divine Light continuous and strong. Because humanity has chosen this strange path, we have existed to speed up the return to love. Our work has been to translate the energies of hate and fear to joy and innocence. The Emissaries have always existed in the areas most affected by violence because it is the tension between the violence of the world and the peace of the Emissaries that enhances our mission. We are not here for Bosnia, but for humanity itself. We have placed ourselves here physically to show the irreconcilable differences between love and fear. One doesn't turn on a spotlight in the daytime. You turn it on at night because it is only then that the light will be seen clearly. Amid the smoke and debris of war comes a light so bright that it cannot be ignored.

"We carry out this mission in secret because it is not necessary that people know we are here. Imagine what would happen if they knew we were here. Until now, they have not been ready to understand what it is we do. But that is changing. We have been the guardians of the human race. Until now, we have waited in the shadows for humanity to be ready to control its own destiny. There are now enough enlightened minds to make this possible. The shift from fear to love will be easy if those who have accepted love step forward and act as stewards to this awakening. Knowing about the work of the Emissaries will speed up this movement. When humanity chooses to accept freedom over bondage, our job will be done. This is what you must communicate to the world, Jimmy."

He stood up and motioned for me to follow him. He walked over to the hut and opened the door. I followed him inside. It was a tiny, one-room hut. In one corner stood a single bed, and in the opposite, a small table with a chair. Beside the bed was a nightstand, and next to the stand was another wooden chair. A kerosene lantern sat on the table. There were no books or anything else of a personal nature in the room. The walls were bare, and aside from the door, a single window provided the only opening.

"This is my home," he said. "Here is everything I own. My entire existence is focused on one thing—extending Divine Light. The meditation session lasts twelve hours every day. When it is over I come here. Nothing changes really. The Light channels through me wherever I am. This is my function, my chosen job. I once was no different than you. I had a regular life, I traveled, I had a family. But then I was called. When I sat down in the center of the wheel my old life disappeared.

"Our job is quite literally to save the world, not from damnation but from the result of its own violent thoughts. When you know that, nothing else matters. Now that you are here your life will never be the same again. You have accepted a most important mission, to proclaim the end of time. But the end of time will not come like people think, in a puff of smoke. Time will end in Light because it began in darkness. Time will end when humanity accepts eternity as its home. This is indeed the single most important moment in history. Your function is to help people understand the true meaning of peace so they can choose love over fear."

I sat down on the chair. "I'm not sure why I'm here or what's going to happen, but this whole thing is beginning to overwhelm me. I'm going to declare the end of time? Please don't misunderstand me, this has been a most incredible experience, but I'm frightened to death. If what you're saying is true, then I should be overwhelmed by the importance of this place and what's happening to me. If it's not, then I should accept that we're both crazy. I'm not sure which to believe."

"You will see for yourself," he said. "You won't have to take my word for it for long. Let me explain exactly what is going to happen. Beginning tomorrow you will join us for meditation at midnight. Don't worry about the twelve hours. As you found out earlier today, the Light takes you, you enter into the space of timelessness, and then it is over. You simply need to integrate the twelve rays projected by the Emissaries. This will be done experientially by being present during the meditation. It will be done intellectually by learning the fundamentals of Divine Light. You will come to my hut every afternoon. I will be your teacher. Then you will leave and return to the United States. You'll receive further instructions after you arrive there."

"What about the others I came with?" I asked.

"They'll be fine. They're experiencing the Light just as you are. They will each learn what they came to learn. No one is here by accident, just like you."

He walked over to where I was sitting and put his hand on my forehead. I suddenly experienced what felt like a tremendous flow of water and Light all around me. I don't know how long this feeling lasted, but I was completely immersed in the Light. When it ended I opened my eyes and he was gone.

I stood up and found my way back to the rest of my friends.

I ate an early dinner and prepared to retire early. The rest of the group would join the meditation at six the next morning. I was alone in the house with Snjezana. I told her about my conversation with the One in the Center.

"I am very glad it was you who was chosen and not me," she said, laughing. "I would not want to teach the end of time. I like too many things for time to end just yet."

"I'm not sure I understand or believe all this, Snjezana. But if I think about it, everything I've ever done, everything I've learned has led to this. There was nothing he said to me that I didn't teach in my workshop. But it's a whole different experience when it actually happens to you. Suddenly it's concrete and real, not just a concept. But I'm putting myself way out there. I don't know how I'm supposed to tell people about this place, but I wouldn't believe it if I heard it. Why will anyone believe me? What am I supposed to do, walk up to people and say, 'It's time to wake up. It's the end of the world as we know it'?"

"Yes," she said.

"What do you mean?"

"I mean, that's exactly what you'll say, perhaps not like that, but I know you'll find a way to tell people the truth in a way they can hear you. You're good at that."

"But they'll think I'm crazy."

"The world is crazy," she said. "Since when has the world been so wise? You'll be telling them that they are made of love. Simple. You'll say that heaven is real, and that they can experience it right now. They don't have to die or experience a hundred more lifetimes. That's what everyone is dying to hear. They've just been waiting for someone to say it with certainty. And that's what you'll do. Of course, some people will think you're crazy. But others will understand. Those are the people you're being sent to, I'm sure."

"But why me?" I asked. "Surely there are people a lot more qualified than I am."

"Jimmy, there's something that happens to you when you perform. You become translucent, almost like you disappear. It's as if you become the music and the music becomes you. And when that happens the audience experiences the music in a way they are not used to. It happens to them because you allow it to happen to you. When you allow yourself to be transformed by Divine Light like you do with music, the same thing will happen. People will experience it because you allowed yourself to experience it first. That's how it works. We each have to accept the truth for ourselves before we can extend it. When we extend it, whoever is ready will feel and experience it as well."

I knew she was right. I also knew that the Emissaries were real and that this mission I was being prepared for was real as well. It did frighten me, though. And yet, there was something about the One in the Center that I trusted completely. God only knew what I was getting myself into, but I had jumped in with both feet.

SEVEN

The Power of Light

Native African Prayer for Peace

Almighty God, the Great
  Thumb we cannot evade to
  tie any knot;
the Roaring Thunder that splits
  mighty trees:
the all-seeing Lord up on high who sees
  even the footprints of an antelope on
  a rock mass here on Earth.
You are the one who does
  not hesitate to respond to our call.
You are the cornerstone of peace.

—The Peace Seeds

I awoke to darkness. It was eleven-thirty, the time I would normally be going to sleep. I had only slept about three hours. My mind was far too active to stay asleep. I put on my clothes and tried not to wake the others.

The moon was nearly full that night. The light made navigating the path to the meditation house easy. Ahead of me I saw someone walking. When he got to the door of the building, he stopped and waited for me. It was Toni.

"Hello, Jimmy," he whispered. "You can sit wherever you like from now on. If you need anything just call me in your mind. I will hear you."

We entered the building. The Emissaries were already in place, including the One in the Center. After a few moments of silence I heard a chime being sounded. The attendants then walked around the room and lit the candles, then the incense. Then they assumed their places against the wall. A moment later I heard a low humming noise coming from the wheel. The noise turned into a deep chant, similar to the one the Emissaries ended their meditation with the day before. It lasted approximately five minutes. When they were finished the room was silent. I leaned my back against the wall and settled in. There was not another sound for twelve hours.

It would be impossible to explain what I experienced during that time. Just as I was told, time was not as it normally was. It was as though we were suspended there, beyond time and space. There was an eternal quality to the experience. My mind was clear and still. I seemed to move in and out of the room, soaring at times through the universe, then quiet and serene, fully aware of my surroundings. I barely noticed when the others walked in. Nadina smiled and sat near me. Gordana, Snjezana, and Duro walked to the other side of the wheel. Then all was quiet again. It seemed as if an hour passed. The sun was shining brightly through the sunroof. The room flooded with light.

A short time later my mind began to hear the chant from the morning before. It started quietly, then grew until it was clear. "Seek not peace here, but find it everywhere. Seek not peace here, but find it everywhere." I opened my eyes and once again saw all twelve Emissaries, including the One in the Center, staring at me. Then it stopped. A moment later they began their chant and the meditation ended.

I had lunch with my friends and the attendants. Five women also joined us. I assumed these were the women whose house we had taken. Other than Sonja, it was the first time I had seen any of them. I felt a bit more integrated than the day before. I sat in front of the fire with Toni and Gordana. Gordana had many questions about the Emissaries that Toni was pleased to answer. I was struck by how open everyone was about a so-called secret community. Perhaps it was because it was nearly time for the whole world to know about this place.

I was to meet at the hut of the One just after lunch. Since I had found it by accident the day before I had paid close attention on my return. I had no trouble finding it again. It was set apart from all the other huts and houses. According to Duro, the One—or Teacher, as I came to know him—rarely spoke with other people. I considered it a great honor, then, to have such an opportunity. As I approached the hut I could see him sitting next to the fire. I walked over without saying a word and sat down on the opposite log. He looked up at me and smiled, then stared back into the fire. This went on for at least ten minutes. I was beginning to feel nervous again.

"Today is the first day of your lessons on Divine Light," he said in a low, serious voice, without looking up from the fire. "Pay very close attention because you must learn to integrate all these lessons before you can teach them to others. Remember that these lessons are about energy, not form. Form is the *result* of energy, the result of thought. Without thought form would not exist. When we change the way we think, form changes. This is the essential teaching. Our task is not to change the world, but to change our thoughts about the world. Those words sound familiar, don't they? That's because I am speaking a language you understand. When you teach you must first determine the language your students will hear. It doesn't matter what words you use, only that they be focused on the truth. And what is the truth? Simply this: Love is real because it is whole. Peace is real because it is sound. God is real because it is eternal. What is not eternal, whole, and sound is not real. It doesn't exist and has no consequence at all. Our task is to reveal what is real. As we do this, we reveal the nature of what isn't. It is that simple." He looked up at me again and smiled. "Now we can begin. How was your first full meditation?"

"It was just as you said. The twelve hours felt like two. I didn't feel like I was there at all but soaring off in space somewhere."

"Try to resist the urge to drift away," he said. "Like the Emissaries, your job is to be present. People must see that this teaching is reasonable, not up in outer space somewhere. Too much emphasis has been put on using spirituality as an escape rather than letting it fulfill its function of leading us to truth. You see, the ego can use spirituality for its own purposes just as easily as anything else. That is why it's important to remain grounded, accessible. If you do, then people won't treat this like a fairy religion or a new-age novelty. They need to have faith in the concrete reality of truth, not the quicksand of illusion. Okay? Now, tell me if you saw anything during the meditation. Did you see any colors or energy fields?"

I told him that I didn't.

"That will come in time," he said. "Let's begin with the first lesson. Yesterday I told you that your mission is to help people release fear. This will be the basis of all your lessons while you're here. Fear is nothing more than the self-imposed block to the experience of love. Why is it self-imposed? Because we have chosen to see ourselves contrary to how we truly are. It's that simple. In truth we are the experience of love itself. This is our essential nature. Fear is our attempt to block our vision of ourselves, to not see ourselves as we truly are. Humanity has convinced itself that it is weak, vulnerable, and open to attack. The opposite is true.

What God created has remained as God created it, in the image and likeness of God. What was created whole cannot be divided, but it can be falsely perceived. And this is the role of fear: to perceive perfection as imperfect, and to see what is true as false.

"Do you see how simple this is, Jimmy? In truth you are not your body at all, but a spirit. Being created in the image and likeness of God has nothing to do with the body, but the invulnerability of the soul. We identify with our bodies because we think we are weak, not strong. Even the belief that the body is joined to the soul is not completely true. The soul ultimately has nothing to do with the body, just as you ultimately have nothing to do with the shirt you are wearing. Would it make sense to say, 'I am this shirt and this shirt is me'? Of course not. You use the shirt, just as you use the body. When you are finished using the shirt you set it aside. Humanity's nature is to express itself freely, not to be bound by form, but to be without constraint or limitation. The need to identify ourselves as bodies is the decision to limit what cannot be limited. Freedom is your spirit's truest attribute, while bondage is what defines the body. As a spirit you are free to do whatever you choose, including perceive yourself as a body. But you are never limited to this experience."

"But I am in a body," I said. "As long as I'm in the world this is how I'll express myself. I'm bound to this expression as long as I'm here."

"Think of it like this," he said as he shifted his weight on the log. "Let's say there was once a man who was thrown into a dark dungeon and sentenced to remain there the rest of his life. The dungeon was dark and musty, and the only time he saw anyone was once a day when a massive guard opened the steel door and placed a plate of food on the floor. He then shut the door and went away. The man rotted in the dungeon for years and thought he would go mad. Finally he made a decision. He would rather die trying to escape than spend another day in this cell. He decided he would wait behind the steel door for the guard to bring his food. When the guard opened the door he would attack him, but because he was so strong, the prisoner was sure the guard would kill him. And this was fine. It was better than being trapped forever in darkness.

"The prisoner positioned himself behind

the door. He reached over and braced himself against the metal handle. When he touched the handle something strange happened. It began to turn. The weight of his grip made the handle move and the door cracked open. It wasn't locked. The prisoner didn't know what to do. He stepped forward and opened the steel door a little farther. It made a loud creak. He looked into the hallway and saw the guard looking at him. And that was all. The guard smiled and stepped aside as the prisoner opened the door, walked into the light, and was free.

"Do you understand what this story means? You are that prisoner, and the dungeon is your body. You believe you were sentenced to your body as if it were a prison cell. And yet the only thing that binds you is your belief that the prison cell is locked, that there is a terrible guard making sure you don't leave, and that you must remain there until you die. Change your belief in these things and the door swings open. You are free. You were never bound at all. Your body was nothing more than a self-imposed limitation that kept you from experiencing freedom."

"You make it sound like it's wrong to experience ourselves as bodies," I said to him.

"Not at all. It has nothing to do with being right or wrong. As divine spirits we have the freedom to express ourselves however we choose, including in bodies. And yet the choice to exist within a body has nothing to do with who you really are. Whether we are in a body or not, the question is always: How will we express ourselves—through love or fear? When we live our lives to extend love we are using the body to express who we really are. That is what the Emissaries do: use the body as a vehicle of truth rather than denial. Teaching people to release fear is learning to use the body in a new way. In the past you have used the body as a vehicle of separation, clearly defining the ways you seem to be separate from others. You will now teach people to use the body as a vehicle of union, demonstrating that separation, fear, and death are impossible dreams."

"But what does the body have to do with releasing fear?" I asked.

"You are afraid because you think you can be attacked. Only the body can be attacked. The ego uses the body to prove you are a separate being that is vulnerable and easily conquered. When you are aware of your natural state, or spirit, you know this is not true. You cannot be attacked because you are not separate from anything. Therefore, there is nothing for you to fear. There is nothing outside or beyond you to attack or hurt the real you. The reason you are afraid is because you have forgotten this fact. You have identified with your body instead of your spirit. The goal of releasing fear is to remember your essential self and your spiritual union with all creation.

"Unfortunately, this goal seems far away when you relate to the world of bodies and form. Humanity needs different tools or exercises to remember truth and re-identify itself. Do you remember when I said that fear is nothing more than a block to your experience of love? Your job will be to help people identify those blocks so they can remember who they are. You can do this in two ways. The first is to identify each manifestation of fear, each instance and situation in which fear presents itself, then use a tool or technique to dissolve it. The problem with this method is that it takes a great deal of time to identify each and every fearful thought lurking in each of the dark corners of the mind.

"The second method is to release the foundation of fear, or in other words, your first fearful thought. This is the thought upon which each subsequent fearful thought has been based. This first thought marks the beginning of delusion, the foundation of an illusory thought system that has influenced and controlled your perception of the world, yourself, each brother and sister, and God. Listen closely, Jimmy, because this is the key to the release of fear. The first fearful, untrue, and illusory thought on which every other thought is based is simply this: You are separate from God. In perceiving yourself as separate from God, you have created a world where you are separate from and threatened by everything. And yet if the foundation of fear is false, then so is each thought that has come from that foundation. Take away this belief and everything above it crumbles. Every building has a cornerstone. If the cornerstone is removed then the building cannot support itself. There is no need to release all the surrounding blocks of fearful beliefs you have. Simply release the idea that you are separate from

God and the dream of separation ends on its own."

The fire was beginning to die. Teacher stood up and walked over to the hut. He picked two logs from a pile, then placed them on the fire. Then he sat back down.

"People are unable to understand how simple this is," he continued. "The method you will teach, then, will be somewhere between the two approaches I have described. You will teach people to pay attention to their fearful thoughts, but not to define or identify them. In other words, don't use your intellect to judge your thoughts. Treat them as energy, feel the emotional impact of the thought, then channel the energy in a different direction.

"Let me explain how the Emissaries extend Divine Light. When people stop judging their thoughts as right or wrong, good or bad, we experience them energetically instead of intellectually. The Emissaries use all their thoughts, including the ones you would call negative. Therefore, we are able to use our thoughts fully instead of them using us. Emotions may vary in both intensity and vibration, but it is always our thoughts about those emotions that give them their charge. For example, you may feel anger in one part of your body and joy in another, and anger may feel very different from joy. When you are angry your body becomes tense, and when you experience joy you are relaxed. But when the judgments and thoughts about those emotions are taken away and the circumstances around the feelings are forgotten, they are experienced as energy.

"Let me teach you an exercise. Close your eyes and imagine the happiest, most joyful experience you can remember. Feel the intensity of that memory. Notice in what part of the body you feel the emotion. Do you feel the sensation in your chest? In your head? Forget the circumstances around the emotion. Let go of the details. Don't judge it, but watch the feeling, completely detached. When you have done this, use your mind to move the sensation to the area around your chest, the area you call your heart."

He paused for a moment as I remembered the day my daughter was born. I remembered holding her in my arms for the first time. The nurse told me to be happy she was a girl because a boy is always a Momma's boy, but a girl is always Daddy's little girl. The miracle of life was so strong and alive in this tiny, magnificent creature. It was the most wonderful feeling I ever experienced.

"Now imagine a small door in the center of your chest. Imagine the door opening, and as it opens the energy you're holding in your heart comes streaming out like a beam of intense light. Allow the energy to flow out of you, a brilliant beam of white light. There is no judgment or thought attached to this light, no veil or covering. You are releasing energy, that is all. Do this until the energy in your chest has dissipated."

I felt the light streaming from my chest. The feeling was both physical and emotional. But most of all it was passionate. The less I thought about the experience the more intense it became.

"Your thoughts about an emotion are like a veil which helps you identify and define what that emotion means to you," he continued. "Your interpretation of whether a feeling is good or bad, happy or sad, is a covering that shows your attitude about yourself. Someone who is generally positive will be more inclined to use the veil of joy than the veil of sadness. But behind each of these veils, each of these coverings, is energy itself. This is the actual experience, the essence you are feeling. Releasing your thoughts about the emotion lets you experience the undefined, formless energy of which all creation is based.

"Keep your eyes closed and think of what you are most afraid of. Feel it in your body and imagine it in as much detail as you can. Notice where the feeling is. In your stomach? In your throat? Now let go of the thought, release the circumstance, but hold on to the feeling just as before. Feel it as energy without judging whether it is right or wrong. Now use your mind to move the feeling to your chest and let it increase and grow."

He paused as I moved the sensation from my stomach to my heart. As soon as I released the judgment the energy felt different. The intensity didn't change, but the intent did. The feeling was no different than it was before—full and passionate. Then he told me to imagine the tiny door and release the light. Once again I felt the incredible flow of energy, as if a huge stream of water was flowing out of me. I was invigorated. I cannot say it was a joyful experience. Neither can I say it was negative. But it was energetic and passionate, as if I had expended an enormous amount of psychic energy.

"Welcome to the world of the Emissaries of Light," he said with a smile. "This is what we do every day during session. You see, energy is energy. It is neither positive nor negative. The way you interpret energy is always related to what you value. When you release your values you are able to use all your emotions, all your feelings, to extend energy, or Divine Light. Without value judgments your fearful thoughts are no different than your joyful thoughts. The reason for pulling them into your chest is to balance and purify the light. The heart is the center of compassion and love. The extension of Divine Light is first and foremost a work of love, an extension of your essential nature. It is not an experience of the intellect. In fact, just as you have seen, mental thoughts only get in the way. Releasing judgment means setting your thoughts aside and trusting your feelings. They are the dynamite that ignites Divine Light. When your mind is clear they become a laser beam that cuts through illusion and deception to the truth of creation."

"Is this the Light you asked if I saw during session?" I asked.

"During session the Emissaries focus their feelings to the center of the wheel. We clear our minds and connect with our essential self. We then project the Light, just as you did when you imagined the door in your heart. The Light travels down the spokes of the wheel and is energized by the symbols. It is not important how this happens. What the Emissaries do is unique, but it is not far from what you will teach. The method I described will help people release the fear that is blocking their extension of love, then use that energy to transform themselves. Every time you practice this technique you send a stream of life-giving energy that revitalizes humanity's awakening. As more and more people learn to release their fear and convert it to Light, humanity's shift to the next stage of evolution will happen rapidly. This release from fear is the key, and this is what your teaching will focus on."

He stood up and motioned for me to follow him. We walked through the thick forest, following an unseen path that led away from the community. Teacher didn't say a word as we walked. I wanted to say something but then I remembered what Duro had said about doing one thing at a time. "When you walk . . . walk," he would say. I thought about everything I was learning. It seemed I was getting a crash course on enlightenment, as if I only had a short time to learn these lessons. And so it should be. I didn't know what they had in mind, but I certainly wasn't going to stay hidden in this forest forever. Part of me was thrilled by this opportunity, but the other part was terrified about my lack of control. I couldn't leave if I wanted to. It would be impossible to navigate my way back to the car alone. Even if I could, I couldn't forget where I was. The Serbian Army was only a few miles away and I didn't particularly feel like meeting them along the path.

We walked for more than an hour in silence. Most of this time was spent going uphill. Now and then we would come to a clearing and I could see the valley far below. Where was he taking me? I didn't dare ask. The ground was becoming loose and rocky. I had to pay close attention to where I stepped to avoid twisting my ankle. The air was cool and moist. I took a deep breath and breathed in the mountain air. Then we came to what seemed to be the top. It was a breathtaking sight, with rolling green hills as far as I could see.

"You're in Bosnia now," he said finally. "But then again, that depends on who you talk to. As far as Serbia is concerned there's no such thing as Bosnia. But to the rest, this mountain is right on the border. This is what all the fighting is about, who's on what side of the mountain. Hundreds of thousands of people have been killed or displaced because of a line in the dirt. At least that's what they say. The real reason is because they're afraid. I say one thing and you say something else. One of us must be right and the other must be wrong. Now we're in competition. If you're not willing to admit you're wrong then there's going to be trouble. We both pull out knives and the fight begins. It's all because we're afraid of one another. We're afraid to let all those differences go and stand together. Holding on to fear becomes more important than reconciling our differences."

He took me by the arm and made me stand a few feet away from him. "You're in Croatia." He took a step backward. "And I'm in Bosnia. We're in two different countries. We have different governments and different laws, even though we may be only a few feet apart. We can choose to be friends or we can be enemies. In this case we're friends because we have a common enemy—Serbia. But up until a few years ago we were all the same—Yugoslavian. That's all changed now and we must make new decisions. Sounds insane, doesn't it? The truth is we all do the same thing in more subtle ways when we imagine ourselves as separate from one another. As long as we imagine ourselves to be different, whether in different countries or in different bodies, we can never really get along.

"If you want to bring peace you have to help people release their fear, especially of the one thing we're most afraid of—ourselves. It's time for humanity to remember, Jimmy. It's time for each person to wake up and realize how holy they are. This is what releasing fear is all about. Do we need more lines in the dirt like this one? What we really need to get rid of are the lines we draw within ourselves. We've split ourselves off from everything, simply because we're not willing to see who we really are. The Emissaries have been holding the light for a very long time, but now it's time for humanity to take responsibility for itself. How much longer can we go on destroying one another like this? Fear gives birth to cruelty, but love brings compassion. Which one will we choose? Believe me, Jimmy, that choice is happening right now."

We sat at the top of that mountain for at least an hour. The thing I remember most was the certainty in his voice. Humanity sat on the edge of some incredible awakening, much like Teacher and I sat there, one of us in Bosnia, the other in Croatia. It was like we were in two different worlds. I began to realize, though, that those two worlds were about to merge.

EIGHT

The Secret of Healing

Native American Prayer for Peace

O Great Spirit of our
Ancestors, I raise
my pipe to you.
To your messengers the four winds, and
to Mother Earth who provides
for your children.
Give us the wisdom to teach our children
to love, to respect, and to be kind
to each other so that they may grow
with peace in mind.
Let us learn to share all good things that
you provide for us on this Earth.

—THE PEACE SEEDS

Though the light from the moon was obscured by clouds, I ran down the path to the meditation house. I was anxious to begin. My first lesson had triggered something wide and expansive in me. The twelve hours of meditating were settling deep inside me. The time I spent with Teacher brought it all to life. It was a perfect balance.

I tried to remain as present as I could during that next session. I was determined to follow Teacher's instructions to the letter. Something had already shifted within me, a certainty about this mission and teaching. Each day that certainty seemed to deepen and mature. It was not something I could clearly define, but rather an internal experience that transcended reason, possessing an impeccable clarity. That certainty became the fruit of everything I learned from the Emissaries.

The session went much as it had the day before. The hours slipped away effortlessly. The energy lifted me up and carried my meditation to incredible heights, but all the while I was present, knowing who I was, where I was, and what I was doing. I remembered what Teacher said about seeing light patterns during session. I looked around the room occasionally, wondering what he meant. I was aware of a light haze that seemed to hang above the wheel, the same haze Duro had mentioned before. But this could have been a trick of the light or a cloud of incense. I wasn't sure. When the session was nearly over, I once again heard the familiar chant in my mind: "Seek not peace here, but find it everywhere. Seek not peace here, but find it everywhere."

When session was over I went for a walk through the forest before lunch. I followed the path most of the way, then wandered into the woods when I felt I was far enough away from the houses and huts. The deep peace I experienced during session lasted for several hours. I walked without thinking, enjoying the depths of the silence of my mind. Just then I saw a hut fifty or so feet in front of me. I thought I was past the community's property. I stopped and wondered if I should turn around.

"Hello," a woman's voice said from behind the hut. "You're welcome to come closer if you choose." One of the female Emissaries, an old woman, stepped out.

"I'm sorry. I didn't mean to sneak up on you."

"That would be impossible," she said, smiling. "I'm glad you are here. It is good to meet the one who will bring the teachings of the Emissaries to the world. My name is Kira."

I introduced myself. I couldn't tell what nationality she was by her accent. But like most I had met, her English was flawless. She had sat on the opposite side of the wheel from me during session. Her eyes were like warm blue oceans. They radiated love and compassion.

"You are much younger than I thought you would be," she said. "But you must be a very quick learner to be chosen for this task. There is not much time for you to learn our ways. The time is drawing very near when people will make their choice, freedom or bondage. The truth is that they make that choice every instant. The energy is now gaining momentum, and once that happens there is no stopping it. The change will be seen by some as positive and by others as negative. Like everything, it is a matter of perspective. We see what we want to see."

"Why is it so important that I teach these things?" I asked.

"For two reasons. The first is that people need to release their fear in order to take the next step in this global awakening. The second is that the energy that will be generated by massive numbers of people learning to channel Divine Light will enable humanity to step past the *appearance* of change, to the changeless within them. This is the shift we speak of. It is not a shift into darkness, like most people think, but into light. Light and darkness are really matters of perspective. Most types of owls, for instance, can see clearly at night, less well during the day. Their eyes just don't work that way. The light we speak of is a shift to truth, a step away from the illusion of separation to the reality of unity."

"When exactly will all this happen?" I asked.

"Very soon. Nearly everyone on the planet has noticed the changes, both in consciousness and the environment. Of course the changes in the environment are simply a reflection of the changes in consciousness. The expression of fear is greater than ever, but so is the extension of love. These energies seem to be moving in two opposite directions. The world often feels like it will split in two. But the spiritual awakening you have seen is just the beginning. As more and more people choose to release their fear and live in love, an awakening will occur that the universe has never seen before. It is ready to happen. But the scaffolding must be removed before we are able to see the inside of a most magnificent temple. The frescoes have been painted, but we can't appreciate them until the scaffolding is removed. The process of removing the scaffolding may seem violent and traumatic, but it is necessary in order to see the beauty of the temple. That is why it is so important that people learn about Divine Light, because it teaches them who they really are."

The way Kira expressed truth was so beautiful and poetic. She was to be the only other Emissary I would meet, other than Teacher. I realized that if I were to have time to eat before that day's lesson I would have to hurry. I thanked Kira and made my way back to the path.

That afternoon I found Teacher working in a small garden down the path from his hut in a small, sunny patch. He was clearing weeds with a rake. The rows were straight and orderly. The garden itself was about thirty square feet with tall, healthy plants in every direction. When he saw me coming up the path he set the rake down and stood up.

"Come over and see my garden," he said with the energy of any enthusiast. "The seasons here are not much different from those in the United States. You can see that things grow very well here. I just wish I could get my hands on some tomato plants. That's what I used to grow, before I came here, I mean. There's nothing better than fresh garden tomatoes."

"Tell me about your life before you became an Emissary," I said. "All I know is that you're from the United States."

"That's almost like asking about a past life. When I came here all that disappeared. My family was gone, all of my affairs ended, and I just found myself here."

"But what was it that brought you here?"

"The wheel brought me. It was almost ten years ago, before the war, when this was all still Yugoslavia. I had lived in Ohio my entire life. I had a family, but they were gone by then. My two children were grown and had moved away. My wife was gone . . . she had died five years earlier in an accident. My life was pretty predictable. I went to work, then came home. I didn't have many friends, just an old dog named Sam. I was neither satisfied nor dissatisfied. I simply existed this way for many years.

"I was never a religious person, and yet there was always something within me that felt connected and full. I read all the spiritual classics and had even spent a month in India. It was all very natural to me. Then I began to have a recurring dream about a twelve-spoked wheel. The wheel would spin and try to envelop me. I ran, hid, and did everything I could to stay away from that wheel. Then one day I held still. I had a feeling of incredible peace as the wheel rolled near, then fell on top of me, landing me right in the center. Every night after that my dream was the same, I was sitting in the middle of the wheel meditating. Nothing else.

"Then one day I found myself on a plane to Yugoslavia. I wasn't sure why I was there, only that I was fascinated by the culture and had several friends in the United States from the area. I landed in Belgrade, then spent a week traveling around the country. One thing led to another and I found myself wandering. I didn't know where I was going, only that I felt led and inspired. I ended up here—again, I'm not even sure how. The other twelve were waiting, sitting around the wheel when I arrived. I walked in the room, entered the wheel, and sat down in the center. Nothing was said or done. In that instant everything happened. I didn't need anyone to tell me what it meant or what I was supposed to do. This was the moment I had spent my entire life being prepared for, and when it happened I understood everything."

I didn't know what to say. I related to so much of his story, as if I too were mysteriously led to this place. I had felt drawn to this part of the world for more than a year. I was almost obsessed by the idea of performing in Bosnia and Croatia. The invitation and everything that led up to my arrival at the community was so mysterious. And when I set foot in the meditation building it was as if all the tumblers fell into place. This is what I had been preparing for my entire life. Everything Teacher taught me, the concepts and exercises, it was as if I were remembering them all, not learning them for the first time.

"Of course you feel that way," Teacher said, reading my thoughts. "How could it be otherwise? You were led here just as surely as I was. These are roles we chose before time began, contracts we made with one another and the world. We each have a role or holy purpose to fulfill, but one person's task is never more important than another's. Even though it seems that one job is more essential or pivotal, the fact is we each have the same ultimate task: to remember who we are. The rest are like roles in a play. When we're onstage one character may have more lines than another, but when the play is over we each go backstage and take off our makeup. We're all just actors on the stage of the world."

"So this role, coming here and meeting you, I chose on some deeper level I'm not aware of. Is that what you're saying?"

"What I'm saying is that you choose everything that happens to you. Everything you have ever done—all the events and lessons, even all the mistakes and trials—has led you to this moment. You are here because of your willingness to discover and extend truth. But don't think that your role is more important or essential than anyone else's. Everything you ever do is a step toward your awakening to truth. Notice that I said *your* awakening. Your job is not to wake up anyone else, but to open your own eyes to the truth that has always been in front of you. You cannot truly heal until you wake up and realize that there is nothing to heal. Does that make sense? You will heal by seeing behind the masks the ego uses to hide the truth.

"Imagine that someone came up to you wearing an ugly mask and asked you to heal a terrible blemish on the plastic surface. What good would you do that person if you took out a can of paint and painted over the blemish? The blemish is not the problem, the mask is. Healing takes place when you look beyond the mask to what is underneath. The beautiful face that is underneath is not affected by the plastic blemish at all. But you may not know this until you are able to see beyond your own mask and realize who you really are. Emissaries are people who have recognized the masks they wear and have seen past them. Only then can they look behind the mask of another, without judgment, and point out the beauty that has never changed. This is the true function of healing."

"There's so much talk about healing and enlightenment back in the United States," I said. "Everyone seems to seek what you're saying, and yet most people still seem so unhappy. They read books, go to workshops, even live in places that are meant to teach peace and truth. But so much of it seems to be a distraction."

"Listen, Jimmy, there's no such thing as not getting what you want. You may not get what you think you ask for, but you always get what you want. The ego's job is to distract and confuse you about this. You can use spirituality to deny truth just as easily as to affirm it. This is why honesty is so vitally important. You have to be able to honestly look at your motivations—all the ways you hide behind fear to keep from seeing the truth behind the mask. When you really want peace, then peace is all you'll experience. When you really want love, love is all you will see. The beginning of honesty is looking at what you are experiencing right now and realizing that it is exactly what you asked to experience. This is probably the hardest thing any of us will ever do. We want to think that things happen to us that are totally beyond our control. Nothing is beyond our control. We are victims only to our unwillingness to experience love. Honesty is the beginning of the return to love. It is the first step toward realizing our power as divine spirits.

"Here is a story that will help you understand. There was once a great teacher who had many disciples dedicated to learning truth. One day one of his students came to him and said, 'Master, all I want is to be as peaceful as you. Please give me the secret to your enlightenment.' The teacher stood up and walked away without saying a word. A week later that same student came to him and said, 'Master, all I want is to be enlightened like you. Do not withhold your secret from me.' Again the teacher turned his back on the student. After another week the student again said, 'Master, I know that you have the secret I seek. I will not rest until you give it to me.' This time the teacher asked the student to follow him down the path to the river. The teacher took off his clothes and jumped in. He told the student to do the same. The young man jumped into the river but before he was able to get his feet beneath him the teacher grabbed him and held him under the water. The student struggled and fought, but the teacher was too strong for him. Finally the teacher let go and the student came up gasping for air. After a moment the teacher said, 'When you were beneath the water, what was the one thing on your mind?' The student wiped the water from his eyes and said, 'Getting a breath of air. All I could think about was air.' The teacher then looked deep into his eyes. 'When you want enlightenment the same way you wanted air, I won't have to tell you anything. Then you will tell me.' "

Teacher knelt back down and resumed his gardening. "Grab the spade and help me with these weeds," he said. I picked up the spade and worked carefully around the peppers. We were quiet for several minutes. It felt good to work with the earth and get my hands dirty. This was the simple lifestyle I loved but had forgotten since living in the city. I could see how easy it would be to stay in this place. The world and its problems felt far away, even though we were in the middle of a war zone. It would be easy for me to forget those things. But the Emissaries had not forgotten. Their work did not remove them from the world, but linked them to it in an intimate way.

"The work of the Emissaries can be summed up with three words," he said finally. "Simplicity, Patience, and Compassion. Extending Divine Light is the culmination of these three things. You must begin to embody them yourself if you are to learn these lessons. They are three sides to a single truth. Everything I teach you will ultimately lead to these three ideas. It's important for you to understand what they really mean.

"Take a look at this garden. All three of these truths are embodied here. The plants are so simple—they're common, ordinary, yet each one is beautiful and capable of producing food that will nurture and support us. But for the plant to do that it must follow its own cycle. Every element of the harvest is contained in the silent memory of the seed. Its patience brings forth the food in its own time. And through each of these cycles the plant is nurtured by compassion: You and me kneeling here, talking to the plant, pulling out the weeds that rob it of its vital energy, all this love encourages the plant to reach maturity quickly and produce a healthy, delicious harvest."

"This sounds very much like what the Emissaries do for humanity," I said as I leaned over and carefully pulled out a weed that was tucked between two plants.

"That's right," Teacher said. "It's the same idea. The simplicity of our work is our understanding that the outcome is assured. Everything will end in love because everything was created in love. Our work is simply to speed up an outcome that is guaranteed. And yet this awakening dawns upon the mind only when it has released enough fear and opened its eyes to truth. It is a process that cannot be rushed; otherwise it causes more fear and postpones the awakening. Imagine you've been sitting in a dark room for hours. To step quickly into a bright room would be traumatic. Therefore, the Emissaries patiently lead humanity out of the darkness and into the Light, just as one would lead a child who is afraid."

"Is this what is happening in the world? We're being led slowly into the Light?"

"Remember that these are all just concepts but, in a way, yes. The Light is within you, Jimmy, it is not out there somewhere. You're being led back to yourself. Now here's one that's a bit more difficult: The world is within you as well. All your attitudes, your reactions, the way you see the world, all of this is within you right now. Is there really a physical universe with bodies and buildings and gardens? You believe there is and that is all that's important. Whether this is a dream or an illusion is unimportant if you believe in it. That's where we need to begin—with your beliefs.

"No two people see the same world. Your perception of the world is very different than mine. We don't even see the same physical world. Once again, what we see with our eyes is determined by what we believe. I remember hearing about a study where they raised a litter of kittens in a room with nothing but vertical lines. When they were grown the cats were moved to a room with nothing but horizontal lines. They bumped into the walls, ran into objects, and knocked over everything that was horizontal because they couldn't see anything but the vertical. Everything you see and believe in is there because you believe in it. You have no idea how much you're missing, simply because you don't have a wider frame of reference. And what keeps you from expanding your frame of reference is fear. When you release your fear you begin to see things in a whole new way. What was always right in front of you suddenly comes to life.

"Once again we are back to the release of fear. Do you see how this is the essential lesson? Happiness, joy, and freedom are right in front of you every moment, waiting for your acceptance. You have gone through life wearing blinders, afraid to look around and see what has always been yours. Releasing fear is all that is required to regain your freedom. Everything you have ever wanted is already yours. It's time for people to understand how simple this is."

We worked in the garden for several hours that day. I was happy that he was relating to me so openly, not at all like the mystical, untouchable person Duro made him seem. He was quite funny and easy to talk to. Though he obviously did not want to discuss his past, I was happy he shared what he did. It made me feel closer to him, as if he were real and could relate to me. I left when it was nearly time for dinner. As I walked away he was still on his knees, caring for each plant in the garden as if it was his own child.

The days passed quickly. I had grown accustomed to the lifestyle and schedule of the community, and every now and then I even forgot about missing my trip back to Italy and wanting to go home. Session became the most important part of the day, followed by my meetings with Teacher. The rest of my time was spent alone or visiting with my friends and the attendants. Of all the attendants, I spent the most time with Toni. I loved his easy, likable personality. And though he never pressed himself or what he knew, I could feel his strength and clarity. He was an example of perfect integration. The *Tao Te Ching* says, "He who knows doesn't talk, and he who talks doesn't know." Those words reminded me of Toni. He didn't need to demonstrate everything he knew and understood, and yet it was clear that his mind had already probed the depths of everything I was learning.

One day before my session with Teacher, Toni and I went for a walk through the forest. We walked for twenty minutes until we came to a steep hill. Toni never said a word. He glanced over his shoulder to make sure I was still with him, then began climbing. The hill was filled with loose rocks and thick clumps of grass. The trees were young and flexible, and I used them for leverage when the hill became too treacherous. Toni looked as if he climbed here every day. Before I knew it he was already at the top and was standing there waiting for me.

"I love to climb," he said, not even out of breath. "I come here often. It is very good exercise."

"Where are we going?" I asked when I finally reached the top.

"You will see. I have something I want to show you."

The hill leveled off and Toni was off again. It took me a moment to catch my breath but I didn't let him get too far ahead of me. I could tell Toni was in good shape just by looking at him. He was tall and thin, his short dark hair giving him the look of a strong Croatian athlete. I guessed he was the same age as me, somewhere in his early thirties, but I never asked. He wore a T-shirt and short running pants. The jeans I wore made climbing difficult.

After a few minutes I could hear an unusual sound ahead. The wind was blowing through the trees above our heads, which made determining the origin of the sound difficult. We soon came to a cliff that overlooked the valley. In the distance I could see the top of the meditation building peering out over the trees. Toni grabbed my arm and pointed to the left. There was a beautiful waterfall not far away, cascading off the top of the hill about one hundred feet to the ground below. It was a beautiful sight. Again Toni darted back into the forest and I followed. We walked very fast around trees and brush, going in the direction of the waterfall. The sound grew louder. Minutes later we were standing at the top, ten feet away from the edge of the cliff. The water was almost silent as it approached the edge, falling from the great wall to a thunderous roar at the bottom. We stood there for several minutes enjoying the beauty of the spot. Then he motioned for me to sit down with him on a large rock a few feet away.

"I want to teach you something," he said. "I know that you are aware of the chant the Emissaries are transmitting to you every day at the end of session: 'Seek not peace here, but find it everywhere.' They are sending you a thought. In essence you are reading their minds. When you first arrived I told you that this is very common here. In fact, it is a very important part of my job as an attendant. It is very easy to hear the thoughts being transmitted by the Emissaries because their minds are so strong. I want to teach you to listen to quiet thoughts, the thoughts that you and I might project. I believe this will help you in your work."

I was very excited about this opportunity. I was amazed at the attendants' ability to read thoughts and often wondered if there was any way to develop the skill.

"The first thing you need to learn is the skill of observation," Toni continued. "There are many ways people project their thoughts. Some of the ways are extremely subtle, others are a bit more obvious. For example, most thoughts are accompanied by a physical reaction. If you think a happy thought you smile. If you are sad you frown. There are also many subtle cues we give each other that are not so obvious. If I'm avoiding a question I'll look away. If I'm lying my pupils will dilate. The first step in tuning in to the thoughts of another is to begin observing these reactions."

He took me by the arm and asked me to stand up. Then he led me to an area that had ten trees growing in a straight line. "Do you see those trees?" he asked. "I want you to think of one of them."

I picked the third tree from the left.

"Now, I want you to hold that thought in your mind and stand behind me. When I start to walk, follow me wherever I go."

Without hesitation, and with me walking three or four yards behind him, Toni walked directly to the tree I was thinking about.

"That's amazing," I said. "How did you do that?"

"You told me exactly where to go, not just with your mind but with your body. I actually wasn't listening to your thoughts. I wanted to demonstrate how this is done strictly from the subtle cues of the body. There were several things you did that told me which tree you were thinking of. For example, just before I took my first step you quickly glanced at the third tree from the left. Then your eyes darted away, obviously aware of what you had done. The body doesn't lie, nor does it hold secrets. If you know what to look for you will always know what the person is thinking.

"You try it. I'm thinking of a tree. To make it a little easier you can touch my arm. Don't think about anything, just be aware of my body. My body will tell you exactly what you want to know. Pay attention to the tension, the direction my limp hand is pointing. Open your mind and let it show you what I'm thinking. When you're ready, start walking and I will follow."

I took a step forward but kept my hand on Toni's wrist. There was nothing obvious in what he was doing with his body that would tell me which tree he was thinking of. He walked about a step behind me. I walked to one side of the line, then turned so we would walk past each one. I watched his eyes, felt his arm. Nothing at all. Then suddenly something happened. I'm not sure what it was, perhaps a twitch or a stuttered breath, but I felt something. I stopped at the sixth tree.

"Is this the tree you were thinking about?"

"Excellent, Jimmy. You have passed the first test. You realized that your mind was not able to consciously pick up every cue I was giving you, but when you allowed yourself to observe in an open, nondiscriminatory way, you walked right to it. This is the key: Trust your feelings and let your subconscious mind notice the physical cues. Always go with your intuitive feelings. You have the ability to observe and process a tremendous amount of information, but if you stay with only the information you pick up consciously you will be limiting yourself. Now let's try a more difficult test. I'm going to think of a tree over there in the forest. I've already picked one out. If you follow the same rules as before it won't be any harder. Start whenever you want."

I started walking toward the forest, away from the edge of the cliff. Toni followed as I lightly touched his wrist. My mind was open. I tried not to think of anything but to be automatic, following my intuition. After taking five or six steps into the forest I had a strong feeling to turn right. When I did I felt Toni relax, as if he were glad I had turned that way. I walked slowly, paying close attention to my feelings and any cues I felt from him. A short time later I felt as if we had gone too far. I'm not sure what it was that made me feel this, but when I turned back around I felt relief. Three steps later I saw Toni glance quickly to the right. At the same time I felt led to turn that way. We turned and walked straight for at least thirty seconds. Suddenly I felt a strong urge to stop. When I did I heard Toni take a deep breath. There were three large trees in front of us. I looked at each one of them. When I looked at the third tree I felt a warm feeling in my hand, as if Toni's wrist were getting warmer. Of course this was impossible but I took it as a sign.

"The third tree," I said. "That's the tree you picked."

Toni stepped back and smiled. "You have a natural talent for mind reading," he said. "Perhaps you will be an attendant someday. You did everything perfectly. I could feel you releasing your thoughts and trusting your intuition. Practice this exercise and you'll soon be able to pick up more specific thoughts. It's the same process, release and trust. The more you practice the better you will get."

We played our game three more times before we decided it was time to head back to the community. I was overjoyed to begin learning this skill. I wondered if it would be as easy to read other people's minds. Maybe Toni's mind was as good at sending thoughts as it was at receiving them. I couldn't wait to practice on my friends.

When I got back to the house the others were there, resting. All of my friends had found their own place in the community. Duro was right at home, obviously comfortable with everyone. Nadina and Gordana spent a great deal of time with the women. They helped cook the meals and do various tasks around the community. Snjezana seemed to spend most of her time with the male attendants. This didn't surprise me since Snjezana never struck me as being shy or reserved. She was a powerful and strong woman, and I wondered if she too was being prepared for some role in this drama.

I spent as much time as I could reflecting on everything I was learning from Teacher.

Though I never sensed he was following any logical progression, everything he taught was bound by a single thread. While most of our talks were spontaneous and unplanned, each lesson centered on the release of fear. According to Teacher, when we release our fear the rest happens automatically. Fear paralyzes us and hides the joy and freedom that's always right in front of us. Releasing fear is like opening our eyes. As long as our eyes are closed we can't accept the gifts that are already ours. The more fear we release, the more we can see. It begins with small steps, but each step shows us that the demons and dragons we hide from are illusory. Their seeming reality is based on and nourished by our fears. In the end we walk right through them as if they were mist. There is no battle. There was never a war. The dragons have always been windmills that our minds made large and ominous.

"Fear is the only thing that is standing between you and your experience of love," he said to me one day as we sat beside a river. "It seems you are afraid of so many things, perhaps everything. The ego searches for and finds everything it can to latch on to and make fearful. But the fear was there already. It was already within you. It seems we are afraid of this thing or that, but in reality we are only afraid of one thing—love itself. And because we are in truth the very essence of love, we are afraid of ourselves. We therefore create a false-self, one that is vulnerable and easily attacked. This keeps us from seeing the source of fear, our own mind, and lets us point to an endless number of things that seem to be out of our control in order to justify our fear.

"And what makes you think you don't deserve love? What ever happened that makes you hide from who you really are? Does it really even matter? There comes a time when you get tired of these questions. There comes a point when nothing means anything and you fall flat on the ground and ask for help. You're tired of hiding. You've been defending yourself for so long that you can't hold your arms up anymore. You surrender. You just can't play the game anymore.

"And that's when it happens. Suddenly you open your eyes and see something incredible. Your own holiness and innocence are held out to you, shining in perfection. At that point, you're like the Prodigal Son who finally gets up enough courage to return home. You may remember that his father had been waiting for him. He had forgotten all about the squandered inheritance. All he knew was that this was his son, returning home after a long journey. The son had given up and would have been content to be treated like one of his father's servants, but the father would have nothing to do with such an idea. All he cared about was that the son that was lost had been found, the beloved child that was dead had come back to life.

"This is what happens when we give up and release our fear. How long will we continue to muddle up our lives before we finally realize that there is One who knows exactly what we need to do, and who is willing to guide us every moment? The two keys to the release of fear are surrender and trust. We want to believe that no one knows what we need but us. And yet if we're really honest with ourselves we realize that we're just getting in our own way. All we do is complicate what is very simple. Admit that you don't always know what's best for you. Realize that you've been making all your decisions from a limited perspective. It's impossible for you to know everything you would need to know to make even the simplest judgment. If you're lost in a forest at night, don't walk around and get more lost. Just sit still and wait for the One who knows the way."

"What you're saying is that we don't have any control over our lives," I said.

"That's not what I'm saying at all. What I'm saying is that we have total control over our lives. Everything that happens to us happens by our choice. If that's true, then it is easy to determine whether you know what's best for yourself. Have your choices brought joy or have they brought conflict? If they bring feelings of joy and peace, then you can be sure that you are beginning to realize who you really are. But if they bring conflict and despair, then you have made decisions against your best interest. Admitting that you don't know what to do is the first step. The next is stepping back and giving control back to God or your higher power. How do you do this? Simply by surrendering, by giving up. This is where trust comes in. It's now obvious that you don't know what's best, but now you have to trust that God does, and that God will guide you if you allow."

"I think I understand what you mean," I said. "But what usually happens is I surrender for a little while, then fall right back into the old habit a day or two later."

"That's fine," Teacher said. "At least for that moment you understood what it meant to surrender. Did you experience peace when you did that?"

"Absolutely. *Whenever* I stop manipulating things and just let things happen, miracles occur all around me. Miracles are natural when we're in the flow, I know that. But how do I remember it when I grab the steering wheel again and try to do it all myself?"

"That will happen as you practice remembering. It's okay to forget. You learn from your mistakes. Just don't beat yourself up every time you fall into those old patterns, because that's what reinforces them. When you realize that you forgot for a moment, shrug your shoulders and start again. It's no big deal. Treat it like a game and it won't seem so serious. The more you do this, and the more you practice remembering, the quicker you will return to the flow, and the happier your life will be.

"You were right when you said that something miraculous occurs when you step back and release control. A miracle is nothing more than the spontaneous expression of your divine, essential nature. When you release your fear and relax into this essential nature, miracles happen all around you. And this is how healing occurs as well. When you release fear you are automatically healed, since sickness is the product of a fearful mind. Since you always extend into your world what you think you are, when you accept healing you extend healing. Everything around you is healed and everything that happens to you happens easily, without effort or conflict. As you practice this more and more, you will begin to notice when you have once again seized control. The more you step back the easier things flow. Conflict becomes your sign to relax and let go. The more you trust the easier it will be to release the fear that seems to control your life.

"This river will teach you everything you need to learn. The water follows and trusts the current. It doesn't try to direct itself but allows itself to be pulled easily and naturally to the ocean. The current knows where it is going. That's why it's the current. The twigs bob merrily along the surface and the fish trust everything the current brings. The water is called by what is greater, the ocean where the current both begins and ends. And this is how we are led when we trust our source and allow that source to lead us along to the fullest, happiest expression of life."

Each day there was something new, but every lesson he taught me had the same goal—peace. It wasn't world peace, but inner peace he stressed. Peace in the world is natural when we experience peace within, he said. We fight wars because we're afraid of one another. We perceive conflict and hatred because we're afraid of ourselves. To bring peace to the world without addressing the conflict where it begins is putting the cart before the horse. All this talk about releasing fear was about realizing that we are both the cause and the solution of our own problems. There is only one problem and one solution. The problem is that we believe we're alone. The solution is that we're not.

The days passed and my lessons continued. I felt like I was on a boat floating gently down the river. It was impossible to know there were rapids just around the bend.

NINE

The Offensive Begins

Muslim Prayer for Peace

In the name of Allah,
the beneficent, the merciful.
Praise be to the Lord of the
Universe who has created us and
made us into tribes and nations.
That we may know each other, not that
we may despise each other.
If the enemy incline towards peace, do
thou also incline towards peace, and
trust God, for the Lord is the one that
heareth and knoweth all things.

And the servants of God,
Most Gracious are those who walk on the Earth in humility, and when we address them, we say "PEACE."

—THE PEACE SEEDS

When I woke up at eleven-thirty that night I felt something was very wrong. I couldn't pinpoint what, only a sense of agitated caution, as if something terrible were about to happen. I put on my clothes and walked outside. When I got to the path I could see Toni running toward me. In the distance I heard a strange sound. I stood still and listened. I realized that there was a battle raging somewhere in the mountains to our right. The sounds of bombs and guns shattered the silence of night. The community was nestled in a valley between two long hills, and the bombs sounded as if they were coming from just beyond one of them. Toni walked up and took me by the arm.

"You must hurry and go to session," he said. "All of us, including your friends and everyone else in the community, must be present."

He hurried past me and went inside the house to get the others. I went as fast as I could to the meditation house. When I went inside everyone else, including the women who normally lived in our house, were already there. The Emissaries were sitting in their usual places. When I entered the building the feeling of caution disappeared. I had the thought that as long as we were there nothing would happen. A few minutes later Nadina, Gordana, Snjezana, and Duro arrived. They sat down not far from me. When Nadina passed I caught a look of fear on her face. Everything became very quiet. Moments later the Emissaries began their opening chant.

All through the night I could hear the explosions in the distance. At first they seemed muffled and far away. As time went by it seemed as if they were getting clearer, and closer. Could the Croatian offensive have already begun? If it had, then we were in the worst possible position, caught somewhere in the middle, directly in the path of both armies. I had a difficult time quieting my mind and meditating. The explosions were not constant or steady. Fifteen minutes would go by with no sound at all, then suddenly there would be five or six blasts. This happened whenever I was about to sink deep inside myself. The hours slipped by slowly. The silence of the room held little relief.

I thought about what the woman at the American embassy had told me. This was a dangerous time to be in the country, especially tucked somewhere near the border of Croatia and Bosnia. She had said the Croatian Army was planning to retake land lost at the beginning of the war. I had heard talk of this many times. The Croats seemed anxious to show their strength, and the depths of hatred between Croatia and Serbia ran deep.

The sun streamed through the skylight about six o'clock. Two hours went by with no explosions. I could hear the sound of singing birds coming through the open door. Occasionally, the sound of a distant explosion broke the silence, but otherwise things were quiet. A few minutes before noon the mental chant began. Then the Emissaries prayed their closing chant, and session ended. They filed out of the building and the rest of us followed. It was a beautiful day. The sun was warm and bright, and a slight breeze rushed through the trees. Whatever had happened the night before seemed over. We followed the attendants to our house to prepare for lunch.

Toni said that there had not been fighting in those hills for several years. The whole region was controlled by the Serbs. There were two nearby towns, about ten miles away, that were of great importance to the Serbs. It was said that many heavy weapons and artillery had been brought in to defend the area against the threat of Croatia. Everyone knew the offensive was coming, the only question was when.

We ate our meal in silence. I felt the reality of war all around us. Nadina and I sat on the floor eating a sandwich made from garden vegetables. Several people sat at the kitchen table, three more near the fire. Toni sat by himself looking out the window. At first I thought he was staring into empty space, but as I watched him more I realized he was watching the field that led to the path. Suddenly he sat up straight as if he were listening to a sound only he could hear. He then signaled to another attendant who immediately set his plate down and ran out the door. Then Toni went to Duro and whispered something in his ear. The other attendants put their plates down and started toward the door.

"What's happening?" I asked him.

"I'll explain later," Toni said. "All of you come with me, quickly."

We followed him out the door. I looked ahead and saw the other attendants lying on the ground, facedown. Toni motioned for us to do the same. He told us to lie very still and not make a sound. That was all. People were scattered in various places on the ground. There didn't seem to be any logic to their positioning, so I found a place and did as everyone else. I lay perfectly still for several minutes. I could feel the same sense of dread I felt earlier before session. There was no sound except for the wind in the trees. The silence itself was frightening. No one moved. I felt like running, but where would I go? I could tell from Toni's reaction that something was very wrong. I buried my head in the grass and held my breath.

Then I heard something. I wasn't sure what it was at first, but after a few seconds I realized it was the sound of engines coming in our direction. Soon there were voices, many voices yelling and screaming. The engines grew very loud and I could hear the sound of feet coming toward us. I tilted my head to the side so I could see. Three army jeeps had just entered the field about two hundred yards away. Behind them were at least a dozen soldiers with guns, running as if they were being chased. They were headed straight for the house. I couldn't move. These were Bosnian Serbs in retreat. If they saw us we would surely be killed. And there was no way they couldn't see us.

I couldn't move. I knew there was nothing I could do, just lie on the ground and wait for them to run right over us. I had heard many stories of the atrocities the Serbian Army had committed against civilians. At that moment there seemed to be only one possible outcome—in a few seconds they would see the house, then the group of us on the ground. Since they were in retreat, possibly being pursued, there wouldn't be time for discussion. We would be killed—quickly, I hoped. I thought of running into the forest. At least I wouldn't be lying on the ground waiting for them. And though there seemed to be no way out, no possibility of escape, there was also a sense of peace all around me, as if I knew we were safe. I opened my eyes again. The soldiers were halfway across the field coming right for us. I watched them, completely detached. Whatever would happen would happen. I had no control. I looked over at Nadina. She looked like she was dead. No one moved or breathed. In a few seconds they would be there. There was nothing we could do but wait.

Suddenly, without warning, the jeeps swerved forty-five degrees to the right. The soldiers followed, and a moment later they disappeared into the woods. I watched in disbelief. Sweat poured off my face and my heart pounded. What made them turn like they did? They were no more than fifty feet away from us. I could actually smell the exhaust from the jeeps. They obviously didn't see us. But that was impossible. The house is clearly visible from the far end of the field.

They had come so close that I could hear the soldiers' breath as they ran. This frightened me. I knew something had happened that I didn't understand.

I wasn't sure if it was over. I turned my head to see if Toni had moved. He hadn't. Everyone was perfectly still. I thought about how lucky it was that the soldiers veered to the right. If they had gone in the opposite direction they would have run right into the huts. I then remembered when we first arrived at the community: We had crossed more than half of the field and I had not seen a thing. Duro asked us to remain perfectly still, and then I saw it. It was as if it appeared from nowhere. It was only at that moment, when I actually knew it was there, that it seemed impossible that anyone could come as close as the soldiers had without seeing us. I could feel my temples beating against the cold ground. I was finally in the middle of the conflict, in the midst of the war. It felt unreal, almost like I was watching a movie and I wasn't there at all. But I was. The feeling of terror had not left, and I knew we were still not safe. Hardest of all was the feeling of helplessness. I was paralyzed, unable to move. When Toni said to lay perfectly still there was a seriousness in his voice that I had not heard before. I took short, quick breaths. There was nothing any of us could do until Toni gave the signal. The minutes felt like hours.

The sound of nearby explosions returned. A battle was raging on the other side of one of the hills. I felt like we were in the middle, caught between both sides. A few minutes later I heard the sound of a helicopter in the distance. At first it blended in with the explosions, but then it became clear, as if it was coming closer. It was headed in our direction. I didn't dare look this time. If the soldiers didn't see the buildings a helicopter certainly would. The sound grew louder. I was sure it had seen us. I heard it directly above us, no more than fifty feet above our heads. At first I thought it had stopped and hovered near the meditation building. I looked up and saw it flash past us. It flew over and was gone. My whole body shook. The sound of the helicopter had nearly pushed me over the edge. It took every ounce of restraint I had in me to keep from running into the house. But I didn't. We lay there for another hour. The bombs continued for a while, then stopped. One of the attendants finally gave the signal that it was safe to stand up. I brushed the grass off my clothes and felt my weak legs tremble as I tried to stand. My friends stood in disbelief. I walked over to Nadina, who looked as if she were about to faint. I held her arm and we went back into the house.

I sat down on a chair and closed my eyes. My entire body ached from fear. It felt as if my stomach was tied in a knot. I took a deep breath and concentrated on the feeling. Then I released the thoughts and judgments that seemed to create the emotion, the thoughts about the soldiers and the helicopter. I followed Teacher's instructions on how to channel fear. I felt the intensity of the fear. Then I moved it into my heart and let it find some balance. When I was ready I imagined the door: It opened and a brilliant stream of white light came pouring out. My whole body began to vibrate. I leaned back in the chair and arched my back as I felt all the fear turn in to piercing energy. Then it was over. I opened my eyes and felt invigorated. The fear melted away and was gone.

After about ten minutes I felt like I was clear enough to think about what had just happened. It was strange to come so close to catastrophe, then have it slide past the way it did. I was still puzzled by what had happened. Why didn't they see us? How could they have come so close and not know we were there? What I just saw was impossible. Toni was sitting across from me, so I asked him what he knew.

"Do you remember when you first came," Toni said, "and it took a while to see us? That's because we let you. We had to make sure it was you before we could show ourselves. Five minutes before you arrived we were laying in the dirt like you just were. When we realized you were friends we let it pass. You see, this is how we have been able to remain a secret community, because you can't see us unless we let you."

"But how is that possible?" I asked him. "Does the place just disappear?"

"Has there ever been something right in front of you that you didn't see? You're looking for it and it's right there, but you can't see it. There's something that's actually stopping your mind from acknowledging its presence. Maybe you don't really want to see it, so you don't. Well, we really don't want them to see us, so something happens to their attention and they don't. Remember, this community has existed for a very long time. Don't you think the Emissaries learned a few tricks in the last thousand or so years? The Emissaries have the ability to project their thoughts great distances. All we have to do is not interfere. That is why we get on the ground and clear our minds. The helicopter flew right over us, but did it see us? Did we disappear? In a way, yes. It seems impossible, but it happens."

Soon after this incident a message came from Teacher that our class would be canceled for that day. It apparently took a great deal of energy to cloak the community. This was the most convincing example I had seen of the power the Emissaries possessed. I spent the rest of that day with my friends. They were as amazed as I was, especially Nadina. A great change had taken place in her since we arrived. Aside from giving up smoking, her attitude had lightened considerably. She was happier than I had ever seen her. Snjezana and Gordana had changed as well. Gordana seemed less preoccupied with the troubles in her life. The community was filled with such vital, loving energy that it was easy to be happy and free.

Late in the afternoon I found Nadina and asked her to come back to the house with me. The others were gone and I wanted to practice the mind-reading exercises I learned from Toni. Nadina was not completely willing to participate. After some time I persuaded her to give it a try. I told her to take her watch off and hide it anywhere in the house while I waited outside. She told me to come back in when she was ready. After I explained what was going to happen I held on to her wrist and took a step forward. I was amazed at the immediate onrush of feelings and impulses. I felt a strong sensation actually pulling me to the left. I walked forward until I heard a voice in my mind that said stop. We were standing in the hallway. The women's bedroom was to our right. We walked into the room and I saw Nadina glance toward the closet. I opened the closet door and reached up to feel a shelf two feet above my head. My hand went directly to the watch, as if I knew exactly where it was.

Nadina stepped back as if she were frightened. "Oh my God," she said. "I can't believe you just did that. I don't know if I should be excited or afraid."

"Why would you be afraid?" I asked her.

"Because you're becoming like the Emissaries. You're going to know everything I'm thinking. I'm not sure if I like that."

"I'm not sure if it works that way," I told her. "If you put a wall up in your mind to hide something, I don't think even an Emissary can see past it. Anyway, I'm not trying to see the intimate details of your mind, at least not today."

"Don't get your hopes up," she said with a smile.

We tried another exercise that was a little more difficult. I asked her to imagine a piece of fruit. I held her hand as she visualized the shape, the color, and the taste of the fruit. I cleared my mind and waited for an impulse. I could feel something forming in my mind, but it wasn't clear. Then I felt a strange sensation in my mouth. I was beginning to salivate. I wasn't sure if this sensation was connected because I still didn't have any clear images. But the salivation continued.

"Is it a lemon?" I finally asked.

"Oh my God," she screamed as she stood up and ran into the kitchen. "This is too strange. I want to go home."

We spent another hour hiding objects and

visualizing fruit. It was one of the most entertaining times I had during my whole trip. The others soon returned and we prepared a simple meal. Everyone was in a good mood, considering how the day began. After the meal it was time for me to get some rest.

The sound of bombs in the distance occasionally broke the silence of the afternoon. By early evening they stopped altogether. The battle was over and I was happy to have made it through the day. I went to bed and hoped the next day would be different.

When I woke up and prepared for session I was happy to hear only the normal sounds of midnight. There were no bombs exploding in the distance, no guns, and no soldiers running in our direction. Whatever battle had been raging the day before seemed over, at least for now. It was impossible to know what had happened. Trips outside the community were rare. The women who maintained the area traveled to nearby towns for supplies only when completely necessary. Most food was grown in small gardens planted in various places around the property. A minimum number of people was needed to maintain the property and feed the members. There was still so much I did not know about the day-to-day activities of the community. I had never seen people live in such simplicity. It was clear that the meditation of the Emissaries was the only focus here. Nothing happened that did not support or maintain their singular goal of fostering peace.

I was anxious to continue with my lessons later that afternoon. The excitement from the day before increased my desire to learn these lessons and then fulfill whatever function was assigned to me. This was my only worry. How was I going to teach this? I was struck by the immense trust the Emissaries had in me, and the responsibility I had accepted was tremendous. I wondered why they hadn't picked someone who could spread the teachings of the Emissaries quickly. I had never been able to expose myself to a large audience before. The one book I had written had only sold a few thousand copies, and the appeal of my music was extremely limited. Perhaps they knew something about me that I didn't. Whatever the case, I felt strange being responsible for something so important. The Emissaries had been a secret society for thousands of years, and it was my job to introduce their message to the world. I had no idea how I was going to do that.

When I arrived at the meditation building, these thoughts disappeared and the peace I felt every day during session returned. This also was strange. I had never been able to develop any disciplined practice of meditation before. I normally had a hard time sitting still for a half hour. And now I was looking forward to getting up at midnight and meditating for twelve hours without a break. This was enough to convince me that something tremendous was happening. There was a feeling of grace all around me. The energy the Emissaries were extending was transforming our lives. I couldn't even imagine what would happen when people learned to do this themselves, and this, of course, was the goal of the Emissaries. After centuries of saving the planet from disaster, it was time to retire and let humanity take care of itself. The Emissaries were the guardians of humanity while it grew and matured. Now, like any person must do when becoming an adult, it was time to go it alone. Humanity was finally ready to be responsible for its own thoughts. I wondered if it was really true.

During session that day I wondered about the question Teacher had asked me about seeing lights or colors. Throughout the meditation I looked around the room in various ways, sometimes squinting, sometimes letting my focus shift and change, wondering what it was he meant. Nothing happened. A few times it seemed as if the haze I saw above the Emissaries began to glow and pulsate, but I decided this was a trick of the light and went back to my meditation.

After lunch I began walking toward Teacher's hut. I was ready to return after my day off. When I got to the hut he was not sitting at the fire as I expected. I looked around the area but he wasn't there. I sat down at the fire, which looked like it had been burning for quite some time. I thought about knocking on the door but I didn't feel it was proper. I coughed a few times in case he was inside resting. Five minutes went by and nothing happened. I stood up and walked toward the house a few steps, then coughed again.

"Do you have a cold?"

He was sitting to the left of the door on a large rock a few feet in front of me. The fire was no more than fifteen or twenty feet away from the hut. Had he been there all along? It would have been impossible not to see him. Was this another demonstration of the same trick that kept the soldiers from seeing us?

"Of course it is," he said as he stood up. "I wanted you to experience it for yourself, so you would understand. Don't underestimate the skill of one who has mastered these lessons. Call it psychic, or miraculous, or whatever you'd like. It's really very simple. The mind sees what it wants to see. Now, you of course wanted to see me. Why didn't you then? Because I was able to recognize that our minds are really joined, not separate. In a sense, there is only one mind expressing itself in a multitude of individual ways. I 'saw' my mind as one with yours, then suggested that you really didn't want to see me. This is of course a simplistic way of describing it. It's actually far easier than that, but it's the only way you have of understanding it right now."

"What about the soldiers?" I asked. "Did you do the same thing to them?"

"Certainly. It is no harder to do it to five people than it is to one. That was certainly not the first time this community has been in danger. Four years ago, at the beginning of the war, the Bosnian Serbs came marching over the mountains like Napoleon. There was absolutely nothing anyone could do about it. At one point they set up a base just beyond that hill." He pointed at the hill over my left shoulder. "Every day missiles were flying right over our heads. After about a week they sent in helicopters and ground troops. The helicopters were flying fifty feet over the meditation building ten times a day. Hundreds of soldiers marched through this forest, practically walking right through the community. But they never saw us. There was never a moment when we were in any danger.

"Remember, One Mind—this is the key. This is also a clue to the secret work of the Emissaries. The soldiers never saw us because they didn't recognize us. Does that make any sense? You see, we accept peace for humanity, that which humanity on its own refuses to accept. How could they recognize us when all they see is war? The Emissaries choose peace, and a choice made in the Power of Divine Light is a powerful choice. Humanity chooses from the ego. This is a very weak choice. Our choice actually cancels out the choice made by the ego. It's that simple. When humanity makes the choice for peace, then they'll work right alongside us."

"What do you mean?" I asked. "I thought you said that the Emissaries will cease to exist when humanity learns to make the choice for peace. You don't mean that people will come to Bosnia and Croatia, do you, or that there will be some new twelve-step group where people sit around a wheel and meditate?"

He laughed at my idea. "Of course not. What I mean is that people need to take responsibility for themselves. People need to choose peace, firmly and finally. As I said many times before, everything we experience is a choice we make. If you want to know what choice you're making, look around you. What do you see, conflict or peace? This is the first lesson an Emissary of Light must learn, that everything they experience is there because they wanted it. When you accept this then you can begin to change your experience. You are the cause and the world is the effect. Change your mind about the world and the world changes."

"You're telling me that there is nothing beyond our control? What about terrible tragedies, like an earthquake or a tornado? If what you're saying is true, then we choose these things. That doesn't make sense."

He poked a stick at the hot coals, stirring the fire. "Of course it doesn't make sense," he said. "Your life is built on the idea that everything is beyond your control. And so it seems until you gather in the reins and choose peace. Then everything changes. Then you begin to experience the power of your choices. That's when you understand."

"But how do we make this new choice?" I asked him. "It's one thing to admit that I've done this to myself, but it's another to choose again."

"I have told you that you will teach the release of fear. When fear is gone, then love dawns upon us naturally. It happens by itself. Everyone will do this in their own way so it is difficult to give a specific process. What I have given you are guidelines, suggestions about how to look at the attitudes that hide and disguise your fear. When we are aware of these attitudes it is like shining a bright light on them. They hide in darkness and cannot exist in the light. They are like shadows that disappear without a trace."

I looked to the left at the shadow my body was casting on the ground. This is what he was saying fear was, a shadow, a false image that we think is real. I wasn't sure I understood what he meant. The fear I felt when the soldiers were coming toward the house certainly seemed real.

"Fear always seems real," he said. "Otherwise you wouldn't give it power over your life. That's why I've given you guidelines to see past it. Two of the guidelines I have given you are surrender and trust. To surrender means to understand that you need help to escape from fear. You cannot do it on your own or you would have done it already. You must learn to step back and surrender to the One who can show you truth. You must let go of your ideas of how it should be done, and accept the vision of One who really knows.

"The second guideline is trust. Once you have stepped back and surrendered, you must trust that you will be given a new answer. Trust clears the cobwebs from the dark corners of your mind that darkness has left behind. The more you trust, the quicker you'll discover peace.

"There is one final guideline I want to give you: gratitude. Gratitude is to your awakening what plutonium is to a nuclear missile. It is the spark that ignites hidden sources of energy and Light, lifting you to whole new levels of joy and peace. You have so much to be grateful for. You have surrendered to a deeper knowing and way, you have put your trust in this new vision of life, and you are grateful for the incredible new perspectives they have shown you. Your gratitude will fill your heart like a balloon, lifting you above the old thought patterns that kept you bound to the earth. It is a natural experience that marks the beginning of your entry into whole new dimensions of Light. I cannot overestimate the power and importance of this final guideline."

"What is it we need to be grateful for?" I asked.

"Everything," he said as he stood up and stepped back from the fire, suddenly excited and animated. "You will be grateful for everything. This is not a trick or a psychological tool. As you release fear through surrender and trust, incredible waves of Light will wash over you. You'll begin to feel joy and peace greater than you even knew existed. It has always been there, you were just afraid to look. But you're not afraid to look anymore, and when you do you will be astonished and amazed. Gratitude will flow out of you like . . . like juice from an orange. Oh, and how sweet that juice will taste! You'll wonder why you never tasted it before. Because you were afraid to, that's why. You were afraid that if you tasted too much joy that you would lose your self, the little idea you have of who you are. The fact is you won't have lost anything. You will have expanded, not contracted. The truth in you could not be held by those little ideas. You're like a glass of water that overflows and spills out over a parched desert. The desert is parched because in trying to contain the water, you withheld it from yourself. But now it flows out and nourishes creation, no longer able to be contained in such a small vessel."

He paced back and forth in front of the fire, his hands moving up and down as he spoke. "You are the water, not the glass. What you are nourishes the universe. You will be grateful for discovering the truth in you, and then you will realize that your only function is to share that truth. Humanity has forgotten itself, and as you and I and others in the world remember our true identity, then share it, humanity itself will remember. Each time the spark of memory dawns on an open mind it sends out a signal to all minds, it creates a ripple that goes through the web of creation, calling it to awaken. Every living creature feels that ripple in the quietest, deepest chamber of its heart. As more and more beings remember, it will be like throwing a handful of rocks into a lake. A thousand ripples will expand and echo within the heart of creation, and within the heart of each creature, that echo will become a pounding drum calling it to awaken, to come alive. And all of this is born through gratitude, Jimmy. A grateful heart is the most powerful force in the universe."

He was like a little child overcome with excitement. Just talking about these things was enough to spark incredible enthusiasm and joy. I could feel it as well. It was as if his joy were overflowing into me, and I stood up and began jumping up and down. Suddenly I was laughing uncontrollably.

"Wow, I can feel it inside me," I said. "I can feel the gratitude and joy building. I feel like I'm going to burst."

"Then burst away," he screamed as he threw his hands up in the air. "You're discovering the passion of waking up. Remembering who you are is not a somber, quiet thing. It's like an electric current that shoots through every part of you. You feel it emotionally as happiness and joy, you feel it spiritually as peace and contentment, and you feel it physically as unbounded excitement and enthusiasm. Your awakening is a whole experience, not limited to any part of you. It is passionate. It's like the sun is exploding. It's whatever brings you freedom and joy. This is what you are, Jimmy. Your fear has been hiding this from you. Why? Because you were afraid you would blow apart if you experienced who you really are. Your ego was afraid you would lose the ability to interact with the world. But it's not true. The ego made the world. The spirit only plays with it like a child. The ego makes everything serious and important. The spirit laughs at everything. Which vision of the world do you want, the ego's or the spirit's? What you're feeling right now is the spirit's.

If you want it you can have it. There's nothing to be afraid of."

There we were, jumping around the fire with our hands up in the air, laughing and screaming. I didn't care if anyone heard us. I felt as if the dam had just broken. The ego had built an enormous wall to hold back passion and joy. Surrender put a crack in that wall, trust put a hole in it, and gratitude blew it apart. The water was flooding every part of me. It washed over me and carried away the fear and resentment that kept me stuck in the ego's desert. It was over now. I knew I could never build that wall again. I leaned back and drank it in.

I saw Duro standing near the meditation building on my way back to the house. He smiled and waved to me. "Would you like to come for a walk?" he asked. I said I would, and we headed in the direction of the field that led to the entrance of the community, the same field the soldiers had entered the day before. We didn't say anything for several minutes. I was struck by the quiet confidence that radiated from Duro. When he talked his words were pointed and sure. There was nothing unclear about him. Our conversations were never filled with pointless, time-filling chatter. If I asked a question he would answer it in concise, well-ordered thoughts. When we were quiet I could feel the vast, deep stillness all around us. I knew very little about his life, only that he had worked as a medical doctor for many years before abandoning much of his practice to explore less traditional holistic methods.

This was how he found the Emissaries. He often left Rijeka to look for rare herbs and plants in remote areas of Croatia and Bosnia. Since discovering the community he had returned many times with supplies and information. During one of these visits he had an unusual conversation with one of the Emissaries. He was told that he would soon be needed to bring an important gift to the Emissaries. This gift would enable the community to begin the final part of its mission—the passing of its guardianship back to humanity. The role they had filled for thousands of years was ending, not because they had failed, but because humanity was on the verge of a spiritual awakening unlike anything that had ever happened before. When Gordana showed him my letter he understood what the Emissaries meant.

He realized that I was the gift they were waiting for, the one who would tell the world about the Emissaries and their work.

I decided that if I were to tell people what I had seen and experienced, I would need to learn more about the history of this place. Previous attempts had proven unsuccessful. Other than the most basic understanding of the community, it seemed as if information was purposely being withheld from me. Duro said that this was because the information wasn't necessary.

"You are trying to understand something that you cannot," he said. "The Emissaries have always existed, but not always in the way you see here. And yet the wheel has remained. How they move from place to place, or how the Emissaries themselves change, there is no way for us to understand. It is as if the Emissaries are the link between time and eternity. Their work is to translate illusion to truth. How is this done? I have no idea. I know about Divine Light, but the deeper level is understood only by the Emissaries themselves."

"Then how is humanity to assume its role if it is beyond our understanding?" I asked.

We came to the far end of the field and

Duro stopped. "Only truth exists," he said. "When you have learned this, then you assume your role as an Emissary. You may not sit within the wheel or find yourself in some remote secret place, but you will join with their minds and join in their work. It has always been this way. These people here are not the only Emissaries extending Divine Light. But a critical mass has almost been reached. When there are enough people on the planet bridging the imaginary gap between truth and illusion, the Emissaries you see here will not be needed to maintain the momentum. This is the maturing of humanity. At that point a global awakening will happen that you cannot even imagine. A new era has arrived, Jimmy, an era for which the world was created, where peace is the rule, not conflict, and love is the law, not hatred."

"How long have the Emissaries been here in Croatia?" I asked.

"They have been in this place for nearly ten years."

"Where were they before this?"

"I do not know. I never felt it was important to know. All I know is that they live and work in the areas most affected by violence. It is easy to see why they are here. For four years we have been fighting this terrible war. The hatred is very deep. The Emissaries have existed in the middle of this conflict, secretly dissolving this hatred and replacing it with hope. I do not know how long they will remain. It does not matter. Everything is about to change, this is clear. And this is why you are here."

"What will happen when this quantum leap happens?" I asked. "Where will the Emissaries go?"

"They will simply be gone. There will be no evidence of them, just as there has never been evidence of them. But through you humanity will know of their gift. Because of your work the final step between humanity and the Emissaries will be bridged. This is why it is important that their mission be revealed, because when humanity learns of this gift it will be able to quickly accept this divine inheritance. The Emissaries are ready to hand this gift back to the child that knew it not. The child is approaching adulthood and can begin to understand how valuable the gift of peace is. The Emissaries have been the guardians of humanity, but when a child is mature it no longer needs a guardian. The guardian then places the inheritance where it belongs. This time is now."

TEN

The Gift of Love

Baha'i Prayer for Peace

Be generous in prosperity,
  and thankful in adversity.
Be fair in thy judgment,
  and guarded in thy speech.
Be a lamp unto those who walk
  in darkness, and a home
  to the stranger.
Be eyes to the blind, and a guiding light
  unto the feet of the erring.
Be a breath of life to the body of
  humankind, a dew to the soil of
  the human heart,
  and a fruit upon the tree of humility.

—The Peace Seeds

Croatia is a beautiful country. Each morning the sun rose above the trees and the moist leaves glistened like jewels. I sat near the door during session nearly every morning. It was always half open and I could see the black sky slowly turn gray, then dark orange, growing brighter and brighter until the whole area was ablaze. By the time we left the building the sun was directly overhead, warming the ground.

Toni and I sat outside on a bench during lunch. The meals were always vegetarian and normally consisted of a wide variety of vegetables, bread, and fruit for dessert. Occasionally the women prepared thick pasta noodles that were either cooked in a soup or served with a light oil sauce. Though simple, the food we ate was delicious and healthy. The Emissaries believed in treating the body with respect, but not to the point that it becomes an obsession. The body is a tool, a vehicle of communication. To become overattentive is to lose sight of its real purpose. To neglect or mistreat it is to forget the ways the body is a gift that helps us extend Divine Light. Life in the Emissary community was completely balanced between the needs of the soul and the requirements of the body.

I asked Toni if he had been there when the Bosnian Serbs attacked the area four years earlier. He said yes, and that he had only been part of the community for a year and had not completely adjusted to the rhythm of life with the Emissaries. One day the entire community was called together and warned that the weeks ahead would be very difficult. They were asked to spend their days in silence, communicating through speech with one another only when completely necessary. They needed to build their energy and conserve their strength. A week later the assault began. A base was perhaps a mile and a half away. There was another military base five miles to the east.

"We were in session when the attack began," he said. "It was around three o'clock in the morning and we could hear the rockets flying above us. They were aimed at the two Croatian towns ten miles away from here. We spent most of our time in the meditation building. We ate very little and didn't talk at all. It was very strange for me because I had not been here for very long. Helicopters flew over the community every day. The Emissaries hardly left the wheel and the rest of us spent many days lying on the floor of the meditation building. I was terribly frightened. I wanted to leave and go back to Split, but I didn't. Dozens of soldiers marched right past us. I could sometimes hear their conversations as they walked through the forest. Weeks later we found out that the Serbs had taken over major portions of Croatia. The community was in the center of the battle, and it has been this way for four years. But just like you, I saw that we were protected. As long as we were with the Emissaries it didn't matter what happened around us."

"Has anyone else ever come to visit the community?" I asked him.

"Only those who have been called to play a particular role in the work of the Emissaries. Duro, for example, is very important to us. The Emissaries do a great deal of work on the higher planes of thought, often inspiring people to make important leaps in consciousness. Also, you could say that the Emissaries are the physical counterpart of a much greater spiritual contingent. You may call these angels or saints. Regardless of what you call them they are able to conduct the same work as the Emissaries, but on much more subtle levels. The veil between the physical and the spiritual is very thin indeed. The Emissaries are able to cross that boundary at will, just as the angelic guides are able to cross to the physical.

"Humanity has such a limited view of things. We tend to judge things strictly by appearance. This is why we are so often wrong. The appearance is just a tiny fragment of the whole picture. It's like trying to understand a novel by reading just one page. The assumptions you make about the rest of the book are bound to be wrong. The Emissaries, in alignment with guides on every level, inspire humanity to let go of its limited perspective and see reality in a new way."

I returned to Teacher's hut at the normal time that afternoon. There was something I wanted to ask him, something I had been thinking about for several days. The strange sense of being protected in the midst of so much violence made me think of another town in Bosnia experiencing a similar phenomenon. I knew that the town of Medjugorje was not far away, the famous town many believed Mary, the mother of Jesus, had been appearing in for nearly fifteen years. In 1981, before Bosnia and Croatia declared independence from Yugoslavia, six children reported seeing Mary on a hill just outside the small town. She was said to have delivered a message of peace, appearing to the children every day and asking people to pray and trust God. She prophesied that a great war would tear apart this area of the world. Many other things she predicted had already come true. Millions of people had flocked to the tiny town, even with bombs exploding in the distant hills. Millions more all over the world had great faith in the apparitions. Church and civil authorities had tried to discredit the children for years. No one was successful.

A month before I left the United States, I was scheduled to perform several concerts in Minneapolis. My entire family lives in the Twin Cities and I stayed, as usual, at my parents' home. One day I went to visit a Catholic church where I was to perform later that fall. I remembered Father Mahon from when I attended Edina High School a block away. He invited me into his office to discuss the concert. We somehow began talking about Medjugorje. He had led several pilgrimages to the town and knew at least one of the visionaries. The oldest of the group, around seventeen when the apparitions began, had married an American woman from Boston. Father Mahon said they were in New England at that time preparing for the birth of their first child. I told him of my desire to go to Bosnia and he gave me their number in Boston, thinking they possibly could help.

When I arrived back in Boston I called and found they had already left. And yet the incident intrigued me. My mother had great faith in the apparitions and had once secretly tucked a book about Medjugorje into my suitcase. I think she felt I had wandered away from the straight and narrow and that only the Blessed Mother could save me now. I had always had a great and deep love for Mary, and though my path did seem to take me outside the normal boundaries of Catholicism, my devotion and love were still strong.

When I arrived at the hut the fire was going strong and Teacher was in his usual place. I sat down across from him.

"I don't have any particular plan, so if you have something you want to ask me this would be a good day." I wasn't even surprised by his psychic tricks anymore.

"Tell me about Medjugorje," I said. "The Blessed Mother has apparently been appearing there for several years and I find it interesting that it would be happening so close to the Emissaries."

He smiled in a way I had not seen before. "What do you want to know?" he asked. "Do you want me to tell you if she's really there? Maybe you want to hear that she's not. Or perhaps you want to know if there's some connection between her and us."

"I don't know what I want to hear. I just want to know what you think."

"Okay. First of all, Mary is indeed appearing in Medjugorje. Are you happy now? The children are not crazy, nor are they liars. But I will also say that things are never as they seem. How much do you know about Mary's message in Medjugorje? Do you realize that she is essentially saying the same things I'm saying to you? . . . Perhaps not in the same way, but the same message. She asks people to turn away from conflict and toward peace. She stresses the need to turn toward God, to surrender to and trust God's guidance. And she asks us to be grateful for the gifts of God, for happiness and love and joy, and the need to give these gifts in order to experience them fully. She may use different words, a more Catholic language, but she's saying the same thing."

"But she also talks about sacrifice and sin," I said. "Those are things you never talk about."

"Now you're asking a different question: Is the phenomenon the children are experiencing the whole picture, the whole truth? To know that, you need to understand a little bit more about how divine revelation works. When I say that Mary is appearing in Medjugorje I mean that the children are witnessing a divine revelation. Divine revelations come to us in many ways. They can be as subtle as an insight inspired by a beautiful sunset. They can also be dramatic like an apparition. The goal of any divine revelation is to inspire peace. Everything that Mary has said in Medjugorje is about peace, and that's why I said it is real. If her message was about revenge, or rose gardens, I would say it wasn't. But this still doesn't say anything about whether the children are experiencing the whole truth.

"The children in Medjugorje are hearing a message of truth, but they will understand that truth only within the limits of their concepts. Our beliefs are like filters that we place between ourselves and the truth. The truth is like a clear beam of light that travels through the filter and changes to whatever color that filter is tinted with. If you're holding a blue filter then the light turns blue. It's still the same beam of light, but the color has been altered by your beliefs. Our religious beliefs are one of the filters we use to understand truth. The children in Medjugorje are Catholic. I'm sure they were given a good Catholic education. They know how to say their rosaries and how to pray the Hail

Mary. Is it any surprise, then, that Mary would be the expression of divine revelation they would witness and that the message they hear would be decidedly Catholic in tone? What if they were Muslim children? Do you think Mary would have appeared to them, or is it more likely that someone they could relate to would appear, maybe Muhammed?"

I remembered a pilgrimage I made to Fatima, Portugal, when I was sixteen. This was the sight of another famous Marian apparition that took place in 1917 in front of three children. I was at an outdoor service that attracted more than 800,000 people, all waving white handkerchiefs as a statue of Mary was carried through the crowd. Though I was moved by the crowd's devotion, I was confused by the way many people used the phenomenon to deepen conflicts with other religions and denominations. Much of the authenticity of the Catholic faith was based on the fact that Mary only appeared to Catholics. Later in my life I learned that apparitions are common in many religions, but only of saints or prophets acknowledged by that particular faith.

"Now, this explanation is not meant to

deny or limit the apparitions, only to understand them," Teacher continued. "As I said before, the fact that the apparitions stress peace and harmony shows they are real. There is without question an insurgence of divine inspiration in Medjugorje, just as there is an insurgence of divine inspiration where you are sitting right now. The mission of the Emissaries is intimately linked to Medjugorje. Most of the reported apparitions of Mary in the last century have been in areas of extreme conflict, just as the Emissaries have always been. During World War I, for example, a time when Europe was in great turmoil, Mary appeared to three children in Fatima. But these were not the only instances of divine revelation, and not all of them involved Mary. Many others experienced a similar phenomenon but within the beliefs of their own traditions."

I stood up and walked behind him. "So what you're saying is that it doesn't matter if it's Mary, or an angel, or the Buddha that appears. That revelation is a gift we receive and interpret according to the beliefs we already have."

"Excellent, Jimmy. Your mind is opening. That is exactly what I'm saying. Just like I said so many times before, there is no separation, nothing outside your mind. You can only see what you allow yourself to see. The children in Medjugorje would be incapable of hearing a message delivered by someone they don't believe in. Imagine if an apparition of the Lord Krishna appeared on that hill instead of the Blessed Mother. A purple man on a hill, that's all they would have seen. But put that same vision in India to six Hindu children and the response would be quite different. The same revelation, a different messenger."

"If you asked my mother, she would tell you that divine revelation only happens to Catholics," I said.

"And that is the filter your mother will see through. If she believes that she alone is right and that other people of different faiths cannot have an equally valid experience of God, then she has put a ceiling on her own experience. This is the problem with concepts, they always have a limit, or a ceiling. The ultimate goal, and this is what you are learning here, is not to have a ceiling at all. This happens by releasing all your concepts. When you no longer use symbols to see God you will see God directly, the reality beyond all symbol and concepts. This is the experience of nonjudgment and it is present in every religion and tradition. It is through nonjudgment that all religions and traditions unite and become one."

His explanation made sense to me. In some ways he was bridging the gap I felt between the way I was raised and the things I now believed. So many of my friends considered themselves "recovering Catholics." I never related to these feelings because I was somehow able to skate across the negative aspects of Catholicism and see the beauty and depth. And yet the message of the Church was still often centered on guilt, sin, and punishment. Everything I was now experiencing showed me something different, a God of forgiveness, not of punishment.

We finished late in the afternoon that day. I had the feeling that my lessons would soon be coming to an end. I wondered what would happen then. What was I being prepared for? What was I going to do with everything he was teaching me? There were still so many questions I had, so many uncertainties. Though I had learned so much in the past week, I felt I still had so much further to go. I saw Nadina as I was walking along the path toward the house. She was sitting beside a pond, staring into space. When she saw me she smiled and motioned for me to come sit with her.

"It's so peaceful here," she said. "I don't understand what's happening, but something is changing inside me. I can feel it. I was so worried before, nothing was going right and I was dissatisfied with my life. Now I realize that I don't have to leave Rijeka to be happy. I can be happy right where I am."

I reached over and took her hand. "You know, Nadina, there have been quite a few times when I wanted to take your hand like this, but for some reason or another I didn't."

She looked up and smiled. "Why not?"

"I don't know. Part of me wanted to feel all those romantic feelings, and another part knew it was perfect just the way it was. I've learned a lot since I've been here, and part of what I learned is that love isn't just about romance and warm feelings. It's about being there for someone in the way they need you, not just the way you want. You and I have been there for each other in lots of different ways already, and I guess that says more about love than anything else. We probably could have had a real exciting time together in Zagreb, but then we would have felt awkward and distant, and none of this would have happened. I kind of like it better this way."

She leaned over and kissed my cheek. "I am happy we are here. Maybe I won't leave this place," she said with a smile.

"What do you mean?" I asked. "What would you do if you stayed?"

"I don't know, but I have thought about it. I have been spending a lot of time with the women here. It has been fun helping them. I'll probably return to Rijeka, but it is very tempting to stay."

"Have you heard any talk about when we'll be leaving?" I asked her.

"I thought you would know," she said. "You are the reason we are here."

"I have a feeling that it won't be long. It seems my lessons are nearly finished and Teacher seems anxious to get me started on my so-called mission. I'm not sure it's a good time to leave, though. What if we walk right into the war? If the Croatian offensive has started there will be soldiers everywhere. Maybe it's not safe."

"It will never be safe," she said. "The war is not going to end in a week. We have to trust the Emissaries. Look at what happened two days ago. I thought for sure we were dead but they never saw us. If they can do that then I'm sure they can get us back to Rijeka."

"Will you come with us when we leave?"

"We will see. There was a reason I came here. We've all been given a tremendous gift. There are only a handful of people in the world that know this place exists. I can't imagine what it will be like when this is over, but it's very exciting. Come on, let's go back to the house."

"Oh, before we go I want you to do something for me."

"What is it?" she asked.

"Imagine a piece of fruit, any kind you want." She hit me in the arm and we stood up to leave.

Snjezana, Gordana, and Duro were inside when we arrived. It was nearly six o'clock, and I would soon need to retire. But I felt a need to connect with everyone, as if our journey would end soon and we needed to complete the experience somehow. Like Nadina, the others had changed as well. It was impossible to be near the Emissaries and not be affected by the energy. I understood why Nadina wanted to stay. I wondered if the others felt the same way.

"If not for my son, I would stay," Gordana said. "My son needs me and I know the point is not about being here physically. I can bring this Light with me wherever I go. But if I could I would stay. Why not? The work the Emissaries do is maybe the most important in the world. And yet it is quiet, removed. Their work is done in secret without prestige or praise. No one even knows they're here. People go on with their lives, never knowing who it is that has been nurturing them, like children who never fully appreciate what their parents have done to raise them. The world may never know what the Emissaries have done, and that's fine. That is why I love these people, because this is the purest form of unconditional love I have ever seen."

"I would not stay, even if I didn't have my daughter," Snjezana said. "The world is ready to stand on its own and I want to be part of that. I feel like we've been midwives to the birth of a new humanity. I want to watch it grow, to see what will happen now.

There will be growth pains and traumas, but if things happen as I suspect, it will be very exciting. I believe I will teach these things I have learned here. Jimmy will go back to America and I will stay in Croatia to extend the Light and bring peace."

Duro said nothing. It was clear that he was already doing exactly what he was supposed to do. He stood between the world and the Emissaries. He watched the changes, saw the growth, and quietly worked to bring the two together. He found me and brought me to them. I still didn't understand how it happened, but it did. I thought I was there for one thing, but that thing grew and took on a life of its own. I was, in fact, doing what I had set out to do—bring peace. Because of Duro I was accomplishing it in ways I could have never imagined.

We talked for more than an hour. There was a sense of completion and I was sure we would be leaving soon. I would miss Teacher. He was more than a guide, he was my savior. He and the other Emissaries had been saving us for centuries. I knew that they would be with me, guiding me when I returned to the United States. The doubts were still there, but there was also the confidence that I would be given everything I would need. The distance between us was of no importance. They would be with me forever, in my heart and in my mind. The journey was just beginning.

That night my dreams were disconnected and confusing. In spite of all the happy feelings I shared with my friends, I was still haunted by my fears. I was alone in my dream, forgotten and laughed at. I tried to speak but no one listened. Everyone I knew turned their back and abandoned me. I was running through a forest as if I was being chased. Then I was hiding in a closet. None of it made sense. I tossed and turned all night, my mind moving from one fearful image to another.

I wasn't able to concentrate the next morning during session. The same questions and concerns were back, not only about being chosen for this so-called mission, but I was also beginning to wonder if I had been set up. I was growing tired of my attitude swings. Whenever I felt completely sure about my mission, fear was right around the bend. I had spent the night before with my friends being grateful for the gifts we had all received, and here I was again, lost in confusion. I was afraid of the responsibility, afraid of the energy I was experiencing, afraid of everything. For a little while I felt that if I had known where we were, I probably would have left. But leaving was impossible. Even if I did remember the way back it was far too dangerous. I had no choice but to wait. As I approached the hut later that day Teacher was sitting in his usual place. I could feel him watching me as I walked up the path. There was no way I could hide my feelings. I sat down on the log across from him.

"Go ahead and say it," I said, without looking up at him.

"What it is you want me to say?" he asked.

"You always know what I'm thinking before I say anything. It's one of your Emissary tricks, isn't it? That means you know how confused I am. I know it doesn't make any sense. I have no logical reason to think that you've misled me or that anything you've said isn't the truth. I guess I'm just afraid."

"What do you want to do about it?"

"I want to leave but that's impossible."

"You can leave anytime you like," he said.

"You're not a prisoner here. If you want I'll ask Duro to prepare to leave right away."

"But what about the soldiers? What if the fighting isn't over?"

"I wouldn't worry about that if I were you. Duro knows what he is doing. I'm sure you'll be able to sneak right past them."

"But what about the others? Maybe they aren't ready to leave yet."

"Are you sure you want to leave?" he asked with a smile. "For someone who is looking for a way out you're sure coming up with a lot of reasons to stay."

I took a deep breath. "I don't know what I want. I don't really want to leave. Of course I believe everything you've taught me. But I'm afraid of what will happen. This is radical stuff, not just about the Emissaries but all these things I've learned from you. It goes against everything the world believes."

"So what is it you really want, Jimmy?"

"I want to stop being afraid. I want to learn this stuff so I can understand it myself. You keep saying that this is all about releasing fear. How am I supposed to teach that if I can't do it myself?"

"Okay, let's try something right now. Close your eyes and take a deep breath.

Now I want you to state your fear as clearly and as specifically as you can. Don't use a lot of words, just say what it is you're afraid of right now."

I thought about what he said. There were so many things swirling through my mind that it was hard to narrow it down to one thing. "I'm afraid people will think I'm crazy," I finally said.

"You're afraid people will think you're crazy for what?"

"I'm afraid people will think I'm crazy if I tell them about the Emissaries."

"Okay, that's good. Now hold that thought in your mind and clear out every other worry or concern. Concentrate on that thought. Identify what part of your body you feel it in. Then imagine that the fear is a ball of energy. If it's in the stomach then imagine a ball of energy sitting there. Do it in whatever way is most natural for you. If you're a visual person then see the color and size of the ball. If you're more tactile then feel the shape and texture. Now let go of the thought that caused the fear. Let go of your worry about being laughed at, of appearing foolish. Forget about all of that and let the fear stand on its own. Watch it, but don't do anything with it. Just watch what it does, how it moves and reacts. Don't give it a thought to hold on to. This is what energizes the fear. Just let it dissolve on its own. If you want to you can move it into your chest and imagine the door in the heart like before. Or you can just let it fade away. Without the thought that created the fear it dissolves by itself. You don't need to fight it or wrestle with it. Just let it leave.

"Now, if you want to, let the fear be replaced by something new. Let yourself feel accepted, understood, and appreciated. That's what you really want, isn't it? Let this new feeling come into your body and see where it rests. Does it rest in the heart or in your head? Now concentrate on this new feeling. Accept it into your being. Welcome it. Ask it to heal any wounds the fear caused. Don't attach any judgment to this new feeling. Just let it come in and be at home. Then open your eyes."

I was amazed at how well this exercise worked. Though I could still feel a bit of residue, the paralyzing fear was gone.

"Like I said before, energy is energy," Teacher said. "When we release our judgments and treat our emotions as energy, they become much easier to release and work with. The most important thing to remember is that energy needs to move. If it's held inside and not released, it grows and attracts more fear. One fearful idea leads to another, and before you know it you're sitting on a whole bundle of negativity that would have been easy to release if attention were given to it right away. Don't be afraid of your fear. The key to staying clear is to keep the energy moving. Don't give it the opportunity to stagnate." He stood up and motioned for me to follow him. "Come on, let's go for a walk."

We walked to the path that led toward the rest of the community. The other buildings were seven or eight minutes away, and I wondered if that's where we were going. We passed one of the women who was working in the garden. She smiled and waved. We walked past the meditation building, then continued on toward the attendants' house. Toni was sitting in a chair near the door and Duro was chopping wood. Neither seemed surprised to see us. This confused me since I was told that Teacher never interacted with the others. I thought they would have reacted more, as if it were an honor for him to come for a visit. I learned that though they honor Teacher and the other Emissaries, they don't treat them like gurus or saints. The Emissaries teach equality, regardless of one's function or job. Holding anyone on a pedestal creates division, and division leads to fear.

We walked past them and went inside. Three of the other attendants were rummaging about the house. They smiled and said hello when we entered. Teacher said something to them in Croatian, I assumed a request for coffee. One of them put some water on and teacher motioned for me to sit down at the table. He pulled out a chair and sat across from me. Within a few minutes several others came into the house and were asked to join us at the table. Teacher asked one of the attendants to go and get the others. Nadina, Snjezana, and Gordana came in along with the other women. Before long all the attendants, the women, and my friends were all in the house, everyone except the other twelve Emissaries. When everyone had a cup of coffee or tea, Teacher began.

"Today is a very important day," he began, pausing every sentence or so to let

Toni translate his words into Croatian. "For many days I have been with Jimmy teaching him about our life here. He has been with us every day in session and has experienced the extension of Divine Light. He has learned about the relationship among simplicity, patience, and compassion, and how to integrate them into his life. He has learned how to surrender, how to trust, and how to be grateful for the gifts of creation. And now he has learned how to confront his own fear, how to watch it and let it go, and even how to extend Divine Light. There is only one more lesson I have to give him and I wanted all of you to be present as well. Without this lesson none of the others make sense.

"The final lesson is about the true meaning of love. I have said before that fear is the self-imposed block to the awareness of love's presence. When fear is released, love is revealed. And yet the true experience of love is beyond anything you can now imagine. It is beyond the thought or the idea of love. It lies past all the images and symbols you have made to obscure love's call. And yet it is closer than you know, closer than your breath or even the silent whisper of love's longing for itself. And what is the secret that love has whispered into your half-closed ear, the distant echo that has haunted you so? Only this: You are the very essence of Love. This very moment, just as you are, in spite of all the preconceived ideas you have of yourself, love claims and accepts you.

"You have forgotten who you are because in your fear of losing love you have withheld that which is your foundation. Love by its very nature is a gift that is freely given. And yet this gift is known only as it is given again. Only when love is breathed from one heart to another is it fully experienced. When love is withheld it is forgotten, and because you and love were born together, you are forgotten with her. She lies hidden within you beside the still forgotten memory of your truest Self. Though asleep and dreaming, she awaits the dawn when her name is called and she is again brought back to life. And the awakening of love is your awakening as well, so intimately linked, all from giving freely that which you are: the full awareness of love's presence. But this awakening requires that you willingly give up all the ways you have tried to limit and contain her. You cannot guide love's path, but if you submit to love's truer vision she will guide you, showing you a new vision of yourself.

"True, or unconditional, love is unaware of the strange demands you impose on your relationships. Love is the same for all. Your attempts to reserve love for specific relationships and then withhold it from others is the very thing that has blocked your vision of love's presence. Give as love gives—just as the sun that gives its light to all who ask, or the sparrow that sings not for the one who listens, but for the song itself. When you give love, love is your reward. When you judge some people as worthy of your giving and other people as undeserving, then it is you who is undeserving; not because you have been judged by love but because you have forgotten love's law.

"You, in your essence, are the fountain of unconditional love. The water you give refreshes the whole universe, for you are not separate from one part of the universe but are intimately linked to all. Let your gift be free, then. Let it flow from you and wash over all those you see, all those who cross your path. Do not think that you cannot still have relationships that are more involved than others. Involvement has nothing to do with love. There will always be those in your life with whom you share the deeper pulse of your thoughts and those whom you do not. But the love you give is the same for each of them. It is but the recognition of the very same life of which you are continually reborn.

"Love is a knowing; a pure understanding. It knows that all things are whole, regardless of their appearance or delusion, and it gives of itself wholly, without judgment, without recognizing the difference between this relationship or that. It understands that there is only one real relationship and it is the one we all share, the Self that is beyond the thought or the idea of Love, the holy encounter of life with life. The secret of unconditional love is that we are all the same, holy beyond imagination. This is what the release of fear reveals. This is what you are all looking for. And this is what you will find when you open your heart to every element of creation."

We sat there for a very long time without saying a word. The silence was overwhelming. I looked up at Teacher and thought I noticed a change. His face began to glow, I was sure of it. The Light radiated from him and all around him. Then it extended to include all of us. We were engulfed in the Light. I cannot describe what this was like because it was beyond anything the world can understand. Several of the women and attendants stood up from their chairs. One of them started jumping up in the air and another began laughing out loud. Soon we were all laughing and dancing, moving with the energy and sharing the Light. I could no longer tell the difference between myself and the others. In that instant I understood everything. I was Teacher. I was the Light. I swam in the ocean of sameness and knew I would never leave again.

ELEVEN
The Escape

Sikh Prayer for Peace

God adjudges us according
  to our deeds,
  not the coat that we wear:
  that Truth is above everything,
  but higher still is truthful living.
Know that we attaineth God when we loveth,
  and only that victory
  endures in consequences of which no
  one is defeated.

—THE PEACE SEEDS

Something had shifted, I knew it. I wasn't sure what, but I knew we had turned an important corner.

I woke up at the normal time and found my way to session. I arrived early for the first time. Three of the attendants were there and that was all. The Emissaries had not arrived yet. A few moments later they entered the building single file in the same order they usually left. Teacher was last. They circled the wheel, and as each one got to their place they stopped. Teacher crossed to the center and they all sat down in unison. A minute later the chime sounded and meditation began. I thought about the wheel and how I wished I had asked Teacher more questions about it. Its symbolism and significance are still mysteries to me. All I know is that this was the single element that bound this group of Emissaries with all the ones before. There was always the wheel. The figures and symbols of the wheel had great significance that made it timeless.

Throughout the night I felt myself experiencing things I had not experienced before. My mind was open and clear, and I felt a strange sensation in my heart and head. I felt as though they were vibrating. It was a powerful sensation that distracted me at first. The pulsing sensation went on for about a half hour, then stopped. I went into a deep meditation. It returned soon after. I was vibrating at an incredible rate. When I opened my eyes it continued and even affected my vision. It was not an unpleasant feeling so I tried to relax into it. Another half hour went by and it disappeared again.

Each time it stopped I found myself able to meditate deeper. My mind fell into a place of complete silence. Though I was present to my surroundings, I was resting in a place so vast, so complete that it felt like I was not there at all. Then the vibrating began again. This time it was stronger than I could stand. I felt my entire body pulsating, but at such a high speed that I couldn't move. I had to stand up or move. It seemed I would explode if it didn't stop soon. I opened my eyes and saw something incredible.

Bright lights streamed from each of the Emissaries. The narrow beams were brilliant and intense, a different color coming from each one. It looked like the light was coming from the area around each Emissary's heart. The beams traveled along the spokes of the wheel to the center, where Teacher sat. The different colors seemed to converge in him, then were directed up through the top of his head through the skylight. When the light came out of his head it was dazzling white. I was stunned and amazed by this sight. All I wanted to do was watch this incredible flow of energy. I moved my head back and forth but it didn't seem to affect the vision. It was as if I were finally able to see something that was there all along.

I learned later that I was seeing the real work of the Emissaries, the extending of Divine Light. The Emissaries around the circle represented each of the twelve aspects of humanity. The color each one projected corresponded with that aspect. The colors moved along the symbols of the wheel and were charged with a mystical force. When they reached the center of the wheel, Teacher would pull each of the beams together and make them one. This purified the Light and made it white.

The Light was then projected into the world, just as I had been told. This was the Light that kept humanity from completely forgetting the truth. It was this energy that canceled out the effect of millions of negatively charged thoughts, keeping humanity straight on the evolutionary track of remembering Divinity.

I sat and watched the Lights. From that moment on I was able to see them whenever I wanted. It was a brilliant display. Occasionally one of the Emissaries would lose energy and his or her Light would begin to fade slightly. When this happened one of the attendants would project a stream of Light to the Emissary, filling the Emissary with energy. This was apparently the main responsibility of the attendants. The vibrating I felt continued, but at a rate I could handle. I was far too excited about what I was seeing to think about anything else. At six o'clock my friends joined us. I wondered if they could see the Light. I finally understood that this was part of what Teacher had been preparing me for. He had said that when I was able to integrate all the lessons these things would happen by themselves.

When session was nearly over the Light suddenly stopped. A moment later I heard the familiar chant in my head: "Seek not peace here, but find it everywhere." Then the closing chant began, and session ended. The Emissaries stood up to leave. As they passed me each one of them smiled, all but Teacher. It was as if we weren't finished. There was still something he and I had to do. I didn't know if I was to meet with him again or not. I hoped it wasn't over because there was still so much I wanted to ask him. I was the last to leave the room. I walked alone into the sun.

We ate lunch at the attendants' house that afternoon. This had been one of my favorite parts of the day, talking to and learning from these people. Each of the attendants had a unique story to explain how they were called by the Emissaries. Most of them had been there for several years. Unlike the Emissaries, the attendants did not make lifelong commitments to the community. They would serve for a period of years, then return to their lives. This often meant carrying on the work of the Emissaries in the world. They became teachers and mentors. Though they kept their knowledge of the community a secret, their role was to teach people to understand Divine Light in order to speed up humanity's evolution.

Toni walked in just as we finished our meal. He asked Duro, Snjezana, Gordana, and me to follow him into another room. He closed the door behind us.

"I have been told to help you prepare to leave this afternoon," he said. "It is important that you begin quickly so you can get to the car before dark."

"Why are we leaving now?" I asked. "I'm not finished learning . . ."

"You've already learned everything you need for now," Toni continued. "Your lessons haven't stopped, they've just changed. If you don't leave now it will be difficult to get you past the soldiers. The entire area is in turmoil and it is very dangerous, but it's a chance we must take. I'm sure you will be safe."

We walked down the path to our house and got our things together. The other attendants and the women came to say goodbye. I was sad to be leaving so soon, so suddenly, especially after my experience that morning in session. We hugged everyone and were quickly on our way. None of the Emissaries, or Teacher, said goodbye or saw us leave.

The hills were quiet as we began our journey. It had been three days since the bombing and I wondered if the Croatian offensive had ended. It was hard to believe it was over. As quickly as it all began it ended, without drama or emotion, without even the chance to say goodbye. Would I ever be able to return? I didn't have any idea where we were, except that we were near the border of Bosnia. I would never be able to find my way back alone.

At about four-thirty we took a short break. Duro said we were still about two hours away from the car so we had better not stay long.

Nadina sat down next to me.

"Why didn't you stay?" I asked.

"Because I'm not supposed to," she said. "I don't know where I'm supposed to be, but wherever it is things will be different. That's what I learned. Happiness is not something that happens to me, but by me. It doesn't matter where I am, the opportunities will always be there. For now I'll go back to the SOS line. Maybe someday I will go to the United States, or maybe Canada. It's not an obsession anymore."

Just as Teacher said, we were each there for something different. I may have been the main attraction, but it was clear that Nadina, Snjezana, and Gordana had changed. Each one of them was more settled and sure of herself. Nadina's face had changed as well. Gone was the tired, frustrated look, the victim who had been forced from her home at gunpoint and told to live in a country that didn't even want her. Now she was at home in herself. Being in the presence of the Emissaries had done so much for all of us.

Duro stood up and looked as if he heard something. He motioned for us to be very still. I thought I heard the sound of motors in the distance. He motioned for us to get down on the ground and keep low. We waited to see if the sound was coming in our direction. I heard the motors stop and for a moment everything was quiet again. We didn't move. I was more afraid than when the soldiers nearly saw us before, when we were still with the Emissaries. Then, though the soldiers were coming toward us, somehow I knew we would be safe. But this was different. We were no longer within the protection of the community. We were on our own in an area thick with soldiers. Even Duro looked frightened.

After about a minute we heard voices that seemed to be coming in our direction. Duro stood up and said we must go quickly. We grabbed our things and began jogging through the woods. I could hear the voices somewhere behind us. I heard someone yell something in Croatian. It sounded as if we were being followed. Gordana did not have good shoes on and was having difficulty keeping up. We had to go slowly so she wouldn't fall too far behind. The voices were getting closer. Sweat was pouring off my body and my heart raced. Duro kept looking behind us, but the forest was thick and it was impossible to see anything through the trees. I knew that he wasn't able to do the Emissaries' disappearing act, so our only chance was to outrun whoever was behind us. But we didn't have much of a chance. I could hear the sound of stamping feet and Slavic voices perhaps one hundred yards away.

We came to a path in the woods. Snjezana took Gordana's arm and helped her run. A minute later the path went off in two different directions. Duro stopped. He looked at the path, then turned around and looked behind us. They were not far away. There was no time to lose. Duro told us to climb down a ravine just beside the path and hide behind a large boulder at the bottom. Nadina, Gordana, and I began climbing down the steep hill and Snjezana stayed behind while Duro gave her the keys to the car. When Snjezana began climbing down the hill, Duro stood alone at the top waiting to make sure we all made it. I wondered what he was doing. Was he planning to leave us and keep running? He sprinted down the path to the right and we were alone in the ravine.

What was he doing? He must be trying to draw them away from us, I thought. Snjezana told me to get down behind the boulder and hold very still. I put my face against the boulder and knelt on the ground. It was barely large enough to hide the four of us.

We were clumped together in a tight ball and I could feel each of my friends shaking with fear. Two minutes later three soldiers came running down the path. They stopped at the fork and listened. I hardly breathed as they looked around, wondering which direction to go in. A few seconds later they ran to the right, the same direction as Duro.

We waited about five minutes until we knew they were gone. Snjezana said that if we followed the path to the left it would lead to the car. Duro was on his own. He had sacrificed himself to assure our safety. We continued on that path for two hours until we came to the field. The car was behind the barn where we had left it. No one had said a word since Duro left us. We were too afraid. We got into the car and drove toward Rijeka.

I was asleep when we pulled up to Nadina's apartment. It was already midnight. The Emissaries would be starting session soon. Snjezana and Gordana came inside. There had been very little talking during the trip, especially about Duro. I didn't know what to do. We went into the living room and sat down.

"We have got to talk about Duro," I said. "Where were those soldiers from?"

"I do not know," Snjezana told me. "They were too far away for me to tell. But there is nothing we can do. Duro must take care of himself now. He is a very smart man and I hope he will be okay. We are safe, and that is what is most important. Now we must decide what to do with you, Jimmy. Before Duro left he told me that we must get you back to the United States right away. He said that things will be dangerous for you here. You have been missing for a week and the government will want to know where you have been. I think my friend Sonja will give you the money for a ticket."

"I don't understand," I said. "How could I be in any danger?"

"Tomorrow you must go to Zagreb and leave," she continued. "I will call Sonja in the morning. She will get us a ticket. Then we will put you on a bus." Snjezana took my hand and tears began to fall down her cheeks. "I will miss you very much, but it must be this way."

"I will miss you too," Gordana said. "But I know this is not the end. From the first moment we saw you we knew you would be in our lives forever. When this war is over maybe we will come to America. But now you must go to finish what has already begun. We have helped you all that we can."

"We will come and get you in the morning," Snjezana said. "Gordana can call the bus station and I will arrange the flight. All of us will try and get some sleep."

Snjezana and Gordana left and I was alone with Nadina. Her mother and brother were asleep. She put on some hot water for tea.

"This has been quite a vacation," I told her.

"Yes. When I get bored again I will call you and you will come back. Things are very exciting when you are here."

"Nadina, do you think I'm ready for this?"

She sat down beside me. "You came here to play your music, and look what happened. None of this could have been if you were not ready. You must trust yourself. Don't worry, you will know what to do. When you return to the United States the people who can help you will show up by themselves. This is real. The Emissaries do exist and we have all been lucky to be part of this story."

We drank our tea then went to bed. I knew she was right. The Emissaries were real. I could never have invented such a story. I still didn't know how I would do whatever it was I was supposed to do, but I knew it would happen somehow. I also knew that Teacher was still with me. That's why he didn't say goodbye. Leaving Croatia would not affect anything. Ready or not, everything he prepared me for was about to happen.

Snjezana and Gordana arrived at Nadina's apartment at seven the next morning. A one-way ticket had been booked for Chicago. The next bus left in one hour. Nadina's mother cooked us breakfast and we relaxed for a few minutes. You never would have guessed from the conversation that morning that we had been through so much in the last week and a half. I was glad to have a few happy moments with my friends before I left. We drank our coffee and ate our breakfast, then everyone walked me to the bus station two blocks away.

As we were walking out the door the phone rang. It was Duro. He was safe at home. The soldiers who were chasing us were Croatian. When they caught up with him he said he was a doctor collecting herbs for his practice. He was taken to the local headquarters, questioned, then released. I spoke with him only for a moment. I wanted to thank him for his faith in me. Then Snjezana said we needed to go.

It was hard to believe I was leaving. I felt so close to these people and had been through so much with them. I knew it wasn't the end. This was the beginning of a very long story. I stood outside the bus as long as I could. The bus driver finally said it was time to go. The four of us stood there crying. I got on the bus and it pulled away. They waved until the bus was out of sight.

Chicago was nearing the end of a long heat wave when I arrived. The jet touched down at O'Hare on schedule and I passed through customs without delay. I was in a bit of a daze that first day back. Things had happened so quickly and I had not readjusted to the old rhythm. Aside from the normal jet lag, I was still recovering from the difference in energy between the Emissaries and the "real" world. There had not been a single opportunity to stop and be quiet since I left the community. I went from being chased by soldiers to hurrying off on a jet to avoid the possible suspicion by the Croatian government. Most of my luggage was waiting for me back in Italy. I had originally planned to return there for a month. The moment I stepped foot in Croatia things stopped going according to plan.

I was expecting one of my closest friends to pick me up. I had left a message for Arthur while I was still in Zagreb but it was impossible to know if he had gotten it or if he was free. I waited outside the international terminal for twenty minutes. He wasn't there. However, this was no sign that he wasn't coming, though, since Arthur was rarely on time. Ten minutes later, he arrived. He pulled up, helped me with my guitar and backpack, then gave me a hug. I hadn't been in Chicago for several months and I was anxious to see my daughter. Arthur had a loft downtown where I normally stayed. It was late and neither of us had had dinner. We found a diner and went inside.

During the trip back to the United States I obsessed over my next move. Who would I tell? How much would I tell? There were no easy answers. I knew I could trust Arthur. He was one of the first people who had introduced me to *A Course in Miracles*, and we had also given several workshops together. I ordered a cup of coffee.

"Some pretty incredible things happened to me in Croatia," I said, then paused.

He smiled. "Yeah, like what?"

"Well, it's a long story. Let me ask you a question: Do you think it's possible that there could be a secret society that has kept the world from destroying itself? I mean, imagine that there is a group of people, not the same people, but a community of people that has been doing a special kind of energy work for thousands of years. The reason they're secret is because their work requires that they live in total seclusion, away from the world. The community moves every so many years, according to where the most violence is. When this happens a new group appears, doing the same work and following the same tradition. They do a special type of meditation that cancels out much of the negative energy in the world, replacing it with what they call Divine Light. What would you say about that?"

I felt like I had just destroyed everything I had learned. I couldn't have given a more ridiculous description. Arthur laughed. "I don't know," he said. "Anything is possible."

"Don't laugh, because I just spent the last two weeks at such a place." I proceeded to tell him about the Emissaries and my journey to the community. He listened intently, knowing that I wouldn't make up such a story. When I was through, he looked calm and accepting.

"So, what are you going to do?" he asked.

"Do you believe me?"

"Of course I believe you," he said, smiling.

"But don't you think it's way out there? I mean, if someone came to me with a story like that I would think they were either crazy or . . . I don't know, just crazy."

"Why would you lie to me? You would have no reason to get off an airplane and make something as unusual as that up."

"But you do think it's fantastic—and you obviously think it makes sense."

"Put it this way," he said. "It doesn't *not* make sense. Who's to say how these things work? You know as well as I do that the Spirit moves in mysterious ways. I've sometimes wondered what was holding everything together. This must be the answer. So what now? What are you going to do?"

"I haven't the slightest idea," I told him.

"Teacher said that I would know when the time was right. Well, the time must not be right. Should I start doing workshops? Should I write letters to magazines?"

"Why don't you write another book?"

"Because I don't do that anymore. I'm a musician, not a writer. My first book went nowhere. It was a lot of fun, but I need a way that will make the whole world know about the Emissaries. I have this incredible responsibility. I don't know why they chose me, but they did."

The food came and the conversation changed. After we finished we drove to the loft. I was exhausted. I wanted to talk more but I couldn't. I fell asleep almost as soon as I touched the bed.

The next morning I took the El to Evanston to pick up my daughter, Angela, whom I hadn't seen since April. She was the reason I flew to Chicago instead of Boston. Besides, it would be nice to wind down before I returned to my active life in New England. I met Angela at the YMCA, where she was attending summer camp. My ex-wife, Linda, worked for a travel agency a few blocks away, so we decided to pay her a visit.

When we got to the office I waited outside.

A moment later Angela brought Linda out with her. I had forgotten to tell her that I had been dared to shave my head while in Croatia. I was never one to back out of a reasonable dare, and Linda was never one to understand why. Her reaction convinced me that I probably shouldn't tell her my story. I also decided not to tell anyone else until I reached some clarity. After visiting Linda, Angela and I spent the day wandering around town. It was exactly what I needed. She spent the week with me at Arthur's. When it was time to leave for Boston I felt a bit clearer, but was still far from knowing what to do next.

I spent the next couple of months living with friends in Boston. I had given up my apartment a month before the European tour and was in no position either mentally or financially to look for another. I had also lost the desire to book any concerts. Though the European tour was a great success, I barely made enough money to cover my travel expenses. The only way I had of making money was by performing, and yet the thought of all the work this would require overwhelmed me. I didn't have the energy for anything. I wandered around town with nothing to do. Before long the little money I had saved was gone and I began falling behind in my child support. My uncertainty about my "function" in life paralyzed me. There was no one to turn to since I had told no one else about the Emissaries.

I became very depressed. A friend who lived on an island off the coast of Maine offered to put me up for a while. This seemed like a good place to escape to. I was tired of Boston and longed to be by the ocean. Each day I walked around the island hoping a wave would wash a bottle onto the shore that would have the answer to all my problems. I was beginning to feel like the Emissaries had made a terrible mistake. Maybe I wasn't the one to bring this message to the world. Maybe I should just forget about the whole thing.

Several weeks went by. I had lost touch with most of my friends and had little interest in anything at all. Walking around the island was beginning to get old. When I picked up my guitar the music was hollow and lifeless. I tried to forget everything that had happened to me. I nearly succeeded in convincing myself that it never happened at all. Or perhaps I was set up. Maybe these people were nothing more than crazy dreamers sitting out in the woods making themselves feel important. I saw what I wanted to see. It was time to forget it all and get on with my life. I couldn't let this craziness destroy me.

Then one night I had a dream. Suddenly I was standing outside the meditation building. It was broad daylight and I wondered if session was going on. I went inside. None of the Emissaries were sitting around the wheel. I looked for the attendants, then my friends. No one. Then I looked to the center. Teacher was sitting there looking at me. He motioned for me to come over to him. I stepped over the symbols and walked to the center, then sat down.

"Are you ready yet?" he asked.

"If you're asking if I'm ready to start, the answer is that I'm beyond ready. I've been wandering around for months waiting for a clue. I've just about given up. Why can't you just tell me how I'm supposed to do this? You obviously know what needs to be done."

"Only you can decide," he said calmly. "It must be your decision. You have so many gifts, Jimmy. It doesn't even matter how you do it. Just begin somewhere."

"I don't know if I can. I've practically forgotten everything you taught me. And yet I have no energy to do anything else. I feel like I'm caught in the middle and can't move. I can't find peace anywhere, whether I'm in Croatia or Chicago or Boston. Everywhere I go there is nothing but confusion."

"Don't look for peace here, Jimmy. But find it everywhere."

I looked up at him. "What did you say? That's the telepathic message all of you used to send to me at the end of session. 'Seek not peace here, but find it everywhere.' You told me that you would tell me what it means, but you never did."

"You weren't ready," he said. "When you were here you thought that the work we do is going to bring peace to the world. You perceived a violent world, then set up the circumstances that would make it peaceful. This isn't what the Emissaries do at all. We don't perceive a violent world. It's that simple. We see a world that is living with the illusion of violence, and we project the truth, an experience of peace that has no opposite. This is the choice humanity has been unable to make for itself. *Our mission is not to bring peace to where it isn't, but to reveal peace where it is hidden.* In other words, peace is all that is real. Even when violence seems to exist, even when war and injustice persist, the Emissaries project the vision of truth that doesn't recognize anything but itself. This is how we save the world, by holding a vision of the world that it is afraid to see, the only vision that is real—that the world is already healed, already whole, and already saved."

Teacher stood up and motioned for me to follow him over to the door. It was a beautiful day, just as it had been during that past summer. I stood beside him, just inside the door, looking out.

"Lasting peace will never come to a world that thinks it has a choice between peace and war. The only choice you every really make is between truth and illusion. When you choose truth you discover that peace is always present, regardless of your awareness of its presence. When you choose illusion it is like closing your eyes to what is right in front of you. And this is what it means to wake up from the dream of separation. It's like opening your eyes. Reality was never compromised by your dream. It remained whole and unchanged while you made up your own world where hatred and fear seemed to have meaning.

" 'Seek not peace here' means do not try to fix a world that was born from the idea of conflict. Look past that vision of the world. Seek peace where it really is, within you. Then extend that peace wherever you are, to whoever you meet. Then the world that was born from conflict will change by itself. It will begin to reflect the new choice you have made, the choice to see peace where it really is. In other words, do not look for peace outside yourself. This is the surest way to never find it. The world and everything in it appears to be 'outside.' Go within, to your deepest thoughts and desires. Seek those parts of your mind that are blocking your experience of peace. When you have discovered these blocks and dissolved them in love, then peace will be revealed—first in your mind, then in the world.

"Do not believe those who tell you that you must change the world. It is easy to see that such attempts have always brought temporary results at best. Change your mind about the world. See the world as an extension of your mind. Find peace and love within and it will automatically project itself outward into the world."

He stepped out the door and I followed him.

"The second part, 'but find it everywhere,' refers to this shift. This is the miracle of enlightenment. When you seek peace where it is, within, then you find it everywhere, even in the world. When you seek peace where it is not, or outside, then it is nowhere to be found. When you find peace within, you are able to see the truth. Conflict may still seem to exist, but you now see past it. This is the function of any Emissary of Light. By experiencing peace as the only true reality, we see it present everywhere, even where conflict and war seem to rule. Then we project that vision to humanity, keeping the spark alive that remembers truth. We do not try to end wars, but to dissolve the untrue ideas that cause war. We see peace even when it is hidden beneath centuries of hate and fear. By experiencing the reality of peace, we overlook the unreality of conflict. This is how the Emissaries heal the world."

We began walking in the direction of Teacher's hut. The dream was completely real, as if I weren't dreaming at all, but back in Croatia. We walked past gardens and the huts belonging to the other Emissaries. I wondered where everyone else was. It was strange to see the community so still and quiet. After a few minutes we arrived at the hut. A fire was burning as usual. We both sat down in our assigned places.

"Seeing peace everywhere is the culmination of all the lessons I have taught you, Jimmy. When you have realized that only God's vision of humanity is real, it will be easy to see past illusions and project truth. Peace is everywhere. You can choose to see peace, or you can choose to see violence, but that doesn't change the truth. Your function is to heal with the truth. Stop trying to bring peace to war. Bring peace to peace and then you'll know what you're to do.

"Do you remember when I told you about seeing past the masks people wear? Our masks are the ways we hide who we really are. You can't heal a mask, but you can heal what is behind it. And how do you do that? Simply by seeing that the face behind the mask is already perfect. It is already healed. Healing, then, is simply helping people take off their masks and showing them who they really are. It is the same in bringing peace to the world. Violence and conflict are the masks the world wears to keep from seeing the peace that lies beneath the surface. You will heal the world by taking off the mask, by showing the beautiful reality that has never changed."

The chant finally made sense. Suddenly I understood everything. This was the key that made all the lessons work. The Peace of God is all that is real. This is the foundation of truth. In that instant I knew exactly what to do. It was all so simple, I couldn't believe I had resisted it. The answer was all around me, whispering the obvious solution into my closed ear. I had made a decision before I even met the Emissaries, and I was determined to stick with it. I suddenly realized that this was what I really wanted.

"That's right," he said to me. "If I had told you what you had to do you would have said the same thing you've been saying. Do what you have to do and the people who will help you will show up by themselves. Humanity is ready for this message, Jimmy. They will believe you, I assure you. They want to believe in the Emissaries of Light. The world has been waiting for people to tell the truth, the truth they have always felt inside them, but that they could never quite identify. Tell them what the Emissaries have done for them. But most of all, teach them what you have learned, that they are ready to take a new step, a step so tiny it will hardly be noticed. And yet this tiny step is a leap past the conflict and fear that has seemed so real for so long. Humanity is ready, but it must believe it is ready. This is your purpose, to declare its readiness. And even when the Emissaries are no longer needed, I'll be there whenever you need me. I am within you, right where I have always been. You will know what to do. You've always known what to do. Now go do it."

Suddenly I was alone. I woke up and sat up in my bed. I remembered thinking before I left the Emissaries that my lessons were not over, knowing somehow that there was a missing piece. But I had to come to the end of my rope before I saw it. I did know what to do. It was suddenly so clear. And I knew I didn't have any time to waste. I got out of the bed, turned on the light, and sat down at the desk. I took out a blank sheet of paper and wrote two lines:

Emissary of Light
by James F. Twyman

People will believe me, I thought. They'll believe because they need to. It was midnight. I wrote for twelve hours straight.

TWELVE

The Story Doesn't End

Christian Prayer for Peace

Blessed are the PEACEMAKERS,
for they shall be known as
the Children of God.
But I say to you that hear, love your enemies, do good to those who hate you,
bless those who curse you,
pray for those who abuse you.
To those who strike you on the cheek,
offer the other also,
and from those who take away your cloak,
do not withhold your coat as well.

Give to everyone who begs from you,
and of those who take away your goods,
do not ask them again.
And as you wish that others would do to you, do so to them.

—The Peace Seeds

A good story never ends. I thought this story was over. I had in fact written the entire book, found a literary agent, sold the manuscript, and revised the final draft when it began to happen. It was like a feeling or a voice I heard that said the story wasn't over. It started slowly, like a low humming noise in the back of my mind, but the closer I got to finishing the book the louder it became. When I finished typing the last few words of the previous chapter it was like a loud pounding drum that I couldn't ignore. Hold the presses, this one isn't over yet.

I felt a tremendous amount of enthusiasm

about the book and decided it would be easier to get it published if I moved back to Boston. There were several people I wanted to have read the manuscript, people I trusted and who I knew would give me good feedback. One of them was David, my friend who triggered this adventure when he gave me the twelve peace prayers nearly two years earlier. When I told him the name of the community, the Emissaries of Light, he told me about a friend of his named Bianca who was a member of a spiritual community with a similar name: the Emissaries of Divine Light. He gave me her phone number.

Bianca agreed to meet me for coffee in Quincy, a city just outside Boston. It was two days before Christmas 1995. I told her about the Emissaries, about Teacher and all the things he taught me, and about the wheel of Light and the twelve-hour meditation for peace. When I finished she could hardly speak.

"You have no idea how close many of the things you just described are to the Emissaries of Divine Light," she said. "There has got to be some connection between the two groups."

We decided to walk to Infinity, a bookstore

down the street from the café, to see what companies publish books similar to mine. There were new-agey, self-help type books, including adventure stories that contained spiritual messages, but nothing that seemed to compare to my experience in Croatia and Bosnia. Bianca pulled out a book she had read recently called *Magic at Our Hand*, by Nancy Rose Exeter, also an Emissary of Divine Light.

"Now, this is the kind of company that should publish your book," she said. "I have a funny feeling about it."

We were standing near the front counter talking when I noticed the woman at the cash register watching us. I assumed she was the owner of the store.

"Did you write a book?" she finally asked.

I walked over to the counter. "Yes. I spent the summer in Croatia and Bosnia and had some incredible experiences. I'm looking for a literary agent. Do you happen to know any?"

"As a matter of fact I do," she said. "A friend named Sandy Satterwhite is an agent. Let me run in back and get her number. By the way, my name is Kathy." She shook my hand, then left for the office.

Bianca and I exchanged a quick look. "I have a good feeling about all of this," she kept saying. "This book is going to come out without any effort on your part."

I waited until the day after Christmas to call Sandy. When I did call I was careful not to tell her too much over the phone. "I was invited to go to Croatia and Bosnia this past summer to perform a concert for peace. While I was there I was taken into the mountains, where I had an incredible experience. I was hoping we could have coffee this afternoon and I could tell you the whole story."

We met at three o'clock that day. When I walked into the café I saw a small blond-haired woman with a wide smile, looking like she was waiting for someone. After a few moments I told her the story. She was more than interested. In fact, she was nearly as excited as I was. She canceled her afternoon appointments and went home to read the manuscript. I received a phone call around nine o'clock that same night.

"Hi, Jimmy, it's Sandy. I've got some great news. As I read the manuscript I flashed on a publishing company out in California I think is perfect for this book. The owners are good friends of mine, and guess what—they're both Emissaries of Divine Light. Anyway, I called the office and Brenda was still there. I told her a little about the story and she was thrilled."

"What's the name of the company?" I asked.

"Aslan. The company's name is Aslan Publishing."

That name sounded so familiar but I wasn't sure where I had heard it before. Then I remembered. "Did they publish a book called *Magic at Our Hand*, by Nancy Rose Exeter?"

"Yes, they did."

That was when I finally trusted everything Teacher ever told me. He had been true to his word.

"Brenda wants me to overnight the manuscript to her. And by the way she talked, I think they're going to buy it."

A week later they did. In less than a month I had written the book, found an agent, and sold it to a publisher. This story wasn't over, of that I was sure. It felt like it had just begun. In many ways it had.

An editor was assigned to edit the manuscript. I called her two days after I received the news. She had already read the first draft and was ready with some suggestions.

"You know, I have to be honest with you about something," she said. "The first time I read the manuscript I wasn't all that excited about it. But everyone else was. I thought maybe I was missing something, so I meditated on it that night. That's when it happened. I realized that this is more than just a book. I can't help but think that you're holding out on me. I have the feeling that there's still more coming."

Her suggestions were excellent. I immediately began the task of revising the first draft. I spent a week rewriting the manuscript. This is when I began to understand what she meant. The book wasn't finished. The closer I came to what I thought was the final chapter, the stronger this feeling became. Then something unusual happened. Several days before I finished the rewrite I had a dream. I don't remember all of the details, only that I was in a large house with Croats, Bosnians, and Serbians all living together in a community that was meant to be a model of peace and forgiveness. The following evening I had the same dream, and then the next. After the third night I knew there was some message I was meant to pay attention to. I decided to call Snjezana and ask if my dream meant anything to her.

"It's funny that you would ask that question," she said. "Three days ago I received a phone call from a poet in Sarajevo who wanted to talk to you. Now that there is a peace accord many people want you to come to Sarajevo to perform the Peace Concert. Also—and here is what is amazing—he lives in the exact community you described, a place in Sarajevo where people do not believe in this war but believe in peace. It is a place where people from all of our countries live, showing that we can live together."

Two weeks later I was on a jet to Venice. I told Snjezana to make sure Duro knew I was coming. I desperately wanted to be taken back to the Emissaries to talk with Teacher. I was sure this was part of the plan. I had come back to the United States to write the book, and as soon as the book was written I was being called back to learn more. I could feel myself living the book as I wrote it. I was no longer simply writing about an experience that had happened sometime in the past, I was now in the book, and I had sucked everyone else into it with me.

The bus from Trieste to Rijeka was just as I remembered it. I called Snjezana from the station to let her know when I would arrive. They would be waiting for me. I sat in the back of the bus and half expected to see the friends I had made on the same route seven months earlier. The bus was barely half full. I sat in the back and put my backpack and guitar above me. This time my passport was in my coat pocket. We passed through the two borders without incident. At the border of Croatia and Slovenia I showed my passport to the soldier who then gave me a thirty-day visa. There was no drama and no suspicion. The guards seemed less agitated, but it was obvious that this was still a country living without peace.

The bus cut along the road that ran south along the Adriatic Sea. It was a cold and beautiful day; the sun reflected off the blue water and hurt my eyes. Forty-five minutes had passed since we crossed into Croatia. We would be in Rijeka in another hour. I was so excited to see my friends again, and for all that I knew would come of this visit. I expected so much. The final act was about to begin.

I could see Snjezana, Gordana, and Nadina waiting at the bus station. The doors opened and I walked outside. Nadina was the first to throw her arms around me.

"My life has been so boring since you left," she said. "Now that you are back I know there will be much excitement. I cannot wait."

Snjezana and Gordana put their arms around both of us. "I cannot believe you are back so soon," Gordana said. "You must tell us everything that has happened to you."

They picked up my guitar and backpack. "Come," Snjezana said. "We will go to eat now and you can tell us everything."

We danced down the busy sidewalk toward the center of town. Minutes later we were sitting in a restaurant that overlooks the harbor, talking and drinking coffee. The boats looked like faraway cities of light moving silently through the water. I told them all about my return to the United States, about the confusion I felt, and about the certainty I experienced when I began writing the book. Then I told them all about the events of the last few weeks, everything that had happened since I finished the first draft of the book. They were amazed but not surprised. They had been with me through so much that these continuing revelations seemed quite normal.

I asked Snjezana if she had talked to Duro. She said that she had and that Duro would meet me the next day. She did not know if we would go to the Emissaries or not. Duro told her that many things had changed and that we must consider these things very carefully. I wasn't excited to hear this. The thought of coming this far and not seeing Teacher troubled me. I was sure that I had been brought back to finish something, and I was certain this included being with the Emissaries one more time. Snjezana said I would have to wait until the next day.

I stayed at Nadina's apartment, just as I had before. Each night we ate, cooked, and talked in the tiny living room, the only room in the apartment that was heated. Her family was preparing to leave for North America in two weeks. They had finally been invited to emigrate as part of the Canadian refugee relief program. I was so happy for them. This is what Nadina wanted all along. Neda and

Ned seemed nervous about the trip. For Nadina it meant the chance to go back to college and live a normal life.

Though the war was at a standstill and the guns were now silent, nothing much had changed in Rijeka. Most refugees had not returned to their homes, and probably wouldn't for quite some time. Those who were from areas still under Bosnian Serb control, like Nadina and her family, would never be allowed to return. Most people seemed pessimistic about the chance of lasting peace. The NATO forces could keep the sides apart, but the real change would need to occur in the minds of the people.

Snjezana said that Duro wanted me to meet him alone in a café not far from Nadina's apartment called the Filodramatica. I wondered why he was being so secretive. We were all included in everything that had happened. I arrived at the café around two-thirty. Duro had not arrived, so I sat down and ordered a cappuccino. There were only a few other people in the café eating and smoking. A few minutes later Duro walked in.

"It's so good to see you again," I said as I stood up and gave him a hug.

"And it is wonderful to have you with us again," Duro said, smiling. "I am not surprised to have you back so soon. Snjezana has told me everything, about the book and all the excitement. It sounds as if you have put your lessons to good use. Soon everyone will know about the Emissaries and their work."

"Duro, I want to go back. I want to see Teacher and the others. I can never find my way alone. I will need you to bring me, right away if you can. I will be going to Sarajevo soon and do not have much time."

"Why do you want to go?" he asked.

"For many reasons. I feel there is still so much for me to learn, so many lessons Teacher didn't teach me. I also feel that that is why I am here, why I felt so led to return."

"But you have already learned everything that you need to know to fulfill your task."

"How do you know that?" I said. "So many things happened back in the United States, all of which told me to come here. And why would I come here if not to be with Teacher? You have to bring me, Duro. Please, I can't come this far and not go."

Duro was quiet for a moment, as if he was making a decision. "Okay, we will go today.

But only you. The others cannot come this time. Let me go home and pack a few things. I will meet you in front of Nadina's apartment in two hours."

Two hours later Duro pulled up in front of the apartment. I left a note for Nadina explaining what had happened. I was sure she would be disappointed. Gordana and Snjezana were at home. I told them that I was sorry they couldn't come along. Though I wasn't sure how long I would be gone I told them to go ahead and begin making plans in Sarajevo. We would make it somehow.

Duro seemed distant and removed during much of the ride. He was never one to engage in light conversation, but I had the feeling he was deliberately hiding something from me. He had been back to the Emissaries only once since the summer—alone. When I asked him about the trip he gave quick answers. Nothing had changed, he said. When I asked him if Teacher had said anything to him about me, he didn't answer. I decided not to press him, figuring I would find out myself soon enough.

We left late in the afternoon and there was no way to make it to the community before dark. When we arrived at the farmhouse it was nearly midnight. Duro explained that the house had been empty for years and that it was okay for us to spend the night. We parked the car behind the barn and brought our things to the back door. Duro told me to wait while he went in through the basement, then came around to let me in. We brought in our packs, then went back to the car to get some blankets and sleeping bags. Duro lit a fire in the fireplace and we were soon ready for sleep. The house was cold and drafty, and the fire did very little to ease the discomfort. I wrapped myself in two blankets and got as close to the fire as I could.

"What's going to happen when we get there?" I asked Duro. "You didn't seem like you wanted to bring me. Is there something happening that you haven't told me yet?"

"I did want to bring you," he said. "But I would like not to talk more until we get there tomorrow. You have already come so far and I want you to finish this journey. Tomorrow you will understand, I promise. Until then, please do not ask any more questions and let's get some sleep."

I lay back down on the hard floor and tried to rest. Though I was exhausted from traveling for the last several days, I couldn't go to sleep. I was worried about returning to the Emissaries. What was going to happen when we got there? Why was Duro being so mysterious? I tossed and turned the entire night. I had come so far and still had so much to do.

We were on the path leading into the forest by seven. I wondered if there were still soldiers in the area. Duro said that there probably weren't, then began telling me the details of when he was captured. It didn't take long for the two soldiers to catch up to him, and when they did he pretended he was picking herbs for his medical practice, as he had mentioned to us on the phone. He had apparently been collecting plants the entire time we were with the Emissaries so he was able to produce the evidence. They said it was suspicious that anyone would be in this area, regardless of the reason. Duro agreed but said that this was the only area where some of these plants grew. Though it was dangerous it was a risk he was willing to take. The soldiers took him to a nearby town and he was questioned for hours. His documents and identification all checked out so they had no choice but to let him go. He even claimed that his car broke down and talked them into providing transportation to a village along the bus route.

"Tell me about the book," Duro said, showing rare interest in something new.

"It was exactly like Teacher said it would be. For months I resisted and was miserable, but when I finally surrendered I was completely confident. So many people showed up, each playing an essential part in getting the manuscript into the right hands. When I finally let go of my fear and began writing, everything happened so fast. It was as if we were running out of time and had to get everything done in a hurry."

"That's true, but not for the reasons you think," he said. "Don't believe that you have to hurry to beat some terrible event or calamity. Things are happening so fast simply because humanity is ready. The only thing that has kept these shifts from happening before is fear. But the fear has been released to the point that the love is able to shine through. Fear is like a dark cloud that blocks the Light. When the cloud lifts, the Light that was always there shines bright.

"Humanity has turned the corner, Jimmy. That is what your book will proclaim. And the return to love will continue to quicken until there is no cloud at all, but only the Light. This is the beginning, and many things still need to change. But it has begun. As more and more people accept their role as Emissaries of Light, the world you once knew will fade away. You and the others who have been called to stand with you will be models of this transformation. You will not stand above humanity to be followed like gurus. You will stand beside them in compassion, bridging the imaginary gap between their fears and what is true. You have accepted salvation for yourselves. And as you accept salvation you will extend it to all those who want it. All the people who have been mysteriously led to help you have answered the same call that brought you here. Each person plays a part, a role that is uniquely his or her own. But in the end each role is the same—to accept salvation and, in doing so, give salvation. The world has changed, Jimmy. It has changed in ways that you don't realize."

We walked for hours. A light covering of snow had fallen, giving the landscape a magical feel. We walked through the forest without saying a word. I tried to pay attention to where he was taking me in case I ever wanted to come back alone. But the route Duro followed seemed indistinguishable, crisscrossing between trees and up and down hills without the aid of a path. It was clear that I would never be able to make this journey on my own.

Then I recognized the long field that led to the community. This was the field the soldiers were crossing when the Emissaries did their disappearing act. I could see the house at the far end. We had made it. I ran ahead of Duro and raced toward the house. It was around one o'clock. Session would have ended and the attendants would be preparing lunch. I ran down the path that led to the attendants. When I came to the house there was no one outside. I threw my pack down on the ground and walked through the door.

The house was cold and empty. The lamps weren't lit and the stove felt like ice. I listened for a sound, anything that would tell me where they were. There was none. I ran back outside. Maybe they were still in the meditation building. I ran as fast as I could but when I arrived it was the same. The door was open and there was no one there. The smell of incense was gone. So was the wheel. The symbols that made up the twelve spokes had vanished. I was alone in an empty, round room.

"This is what I couldn't tell you," Duro said as he stepped inside.

"Where are they?" I yelled.

"They're gone, just like I told you they would be months ago. There would be no sign of them, no trace that they were ever here at all. Do you remember?"

"What do you mean, they're gone? Where would they go? Teacher wouldn't bring me all the way here, then disappear like this. It's not possible."

Duro stepped closer. "You were their gift, Jimmy. You were the final link they needed to finish their mission. For thousands of years the Emissaries have been the guardians of humanity. But now a new humanity has been born. It may be in its infancy but the wisdom you have learned from the Emissaries will help it grow strong. The Peaceful Kingdom is here at last, waiting to be shared. This is what Teacher taught you. This is what all the lessons pointed toward. The release of fear tore down the boundaries that seemed to separate humanity from its source. But that's over now. People are stepping into the Light and becoming Emissaries themselves. It's like a snowball that starts at the top of a mountain, growing larger and larger as it gains momentum. Nothing will stop it now. The entire universe is about to be swallowed up."

"But I don't understand," I said. "Why did you bring me here if you knew they weren't here?"

"Because you had to see for yourself. Don't be sad that they're not here. The Emissaries are within you, and that's where you will always find them. They planted a seed within you that has sprouted. Now you have to go and plant that same seed. This new humanity will not come suddenly upon the world. The seeds you plant will sprout in this place or that, and then those seeds will mature and do the same. Individuals and small groups have already begun to mature, and as they grow further this new vision of humanity will speed, imperceptibly at first, then suddenly it will be there for all to see. The former world will be forgotten and a new era will dawn. The Emissaries are gone because they're not needed anymore. From now on humanity will be able to walk on its own."

"But what about coming here again?" I

asked. "Did Teacher bring me all the way back just to see this?"

"There is still one lesson you must learn, one thing that Teacher wanted me to help you see. He said that this will make everything fit. When you experience this final lesson everything will fall into place."

"And what is that lesson?"

"The final lesson will not take place here, but where you are going—Sarajevo. Something will happen, that's all I know. Just as everything has happened without your effort, so will this final lesson. Everything will happen as it should."

I walked back outside. The sky was clear and a light breeze blew through the trees high above us. I was filled with confusion. I couldn't believe that I was brought all the way back to this hidden and secluded place just to find it deserted. Duro walked out behind me.

"Where did they go, Duro?"

"I don't know. The attendants have gone back to the lives they led before they came here. As for Teacher and the other Emissaries, they simply aren't here anymore. They no longer need their bodies. In that sense they're more available to you than before. Teacher is with you right now, guiding and leading you. You're not alone, Jimmy. You'll never be alone."

I spent the day walking around what had been the Emissary community. I built a fire in the pit next to Teacher's house and sat there thinking about all our conversations. I knew that I would finish in Sarajevo whatever I had started here. I wondered what lay ahead for me there. The fighting had stopped but the hatred was still alive. We slept there that night, then set off for Rijeka early the next morning.

"We go to Sarajevo in one week," Snjezana said when I walked into Suncokret's office. "I just got off the phone with a woman from Suncokret who is in Sarajevo. She has organized a major concert for you with a very famous Bosnian actor. Josip Pejakovic is very popular throughout the former Yugoslavia. He is the director of the peace organization in Sarajevo that will sponsor the concert. But only you and I will go. Nadina cannot because she is a refugee. She is not able to go back to Bosnia. Gordana cannot because she hasn't the money. The bus ride from Rijeka to Sarajevo costs over three hundred German marks. That is because it is very dangerous."

"But isn't it safer now that the war is over?" I asked her.

"The bombs have stopped but the people are still in a terrible situation. Everything has been destroyed and they have no money or food. It is dangerous to be in the country because so many people are being robbed and killed."

That night Snjezana and I were invited to a regional festival called Maskare in Grobnik, a village near Rijeka. The festival celebrates the approach of spring, with four consecutive costume parties beginning each Saturday night at nine o'clock and lasting until dawn. It is traditional to go as a group and dress according to a theme. We were invited by a group of people who spent months making chicken costumes. I was impressed by the effort and time they spent preparing for this party. Two members of their group were not able to attend that week and they offered us their costumes. We rode in two cars and changed into our costumes when we arrived.

The festival was held in a huge open building in the middle of the village. When we arrived at ten o'clock it was already filled. Groups of revelers were crowded together dressed in elaborately creative costumes. One group was dressed as a patch of mushrooms. A group of mimes waved their canes in the air, and twenty men in drag danced about furiously. A five-piece band played Croatian dance music, an odd mix of disco and polka. I noticed an effigy of a soldier hanging on the wall but was afraid to ask the significance. Wine was served in recycled cola and vodka bottles, and cigarette smoke hung above us like a dark cloud. The crowd grew drunk as the night wore on. People began dancing on the tables and sitting on one another's shoulders. Someone lit a flare on the dance floor that filled the room with an eerie, fluorescent light. The smell of sulfur made breathing nearly impossible.

I stuck close to my friends until it was time to announce the winners of the costume contest. The night belonged to us chickens. We were awarded a huge cake, which we shared with everyone at our table. When the contest was over we took off our costumes. It felt good to be out of the chicken outfit. The heat generated by the bodies pushing us across the dance floor made the fact that I was wearing only a T-shirt and jeans quite bearable.

While we were dancing, Snjezana and one of the other women we were with turned me around so they could see the back of my shirt. They were upset with the design, a hand showing a peace sign with the words PEACE BOY written beneath. When I bought the shirt in Chicago, I wondered why the hand showed a three-finger peace sign instead of the traditional two. I figured it was a creative variation on the original and didn't give it much attention. Snjezana explained that this was the sign of a Serbian warrior. It was dangerous to wear such a design in Croatia or Bosnia. I smugly disregarded their warning and continued dancing.

People were getting drunk and loud. I was beginning to feel uncomfortable and hoped we wouldn't stay till dawn as was the custom. It was difficult to push through the crowd when I tried to get to the door for some fresh air. I was near the entrance when someone violently pushed me from behind, nearly knocking me to the ground. I turned around and a very large man grabbed me by the shirt and started screaming. I tried to tell him that I didn't understand but he was screaming too loud. I felt the other men pushing against me. One of them hit me hard in the face and I fell to the ground. I thought they were going to kill me. Five men stood above me screaming and kicking. Just then Snjezana pushed through the group and shielded me from the men. She screamed something in Croatian that made them stop—I assume she said that I was an American and didn't understand. Snjezana threw a shirt around my shoulders and helped me stand up. The men stepped back to let me pass.

The other people in our group saw what happened and grabbed their costumes to leave. Snjezana took me outside to wait for the others.

"Now maybe you will understand that these things are serious," she said. "It may not mean anything to you but these people are so angry. They will use any reason they can find to be violent."

A few minutes later the others met us at the car. They were all sorry about what had happened and tried to explain.

"I am from a city in Bosnia called Doboj," Denisa, one of the women in our group, told me. "That city was taken over by the Serbians but my family continued to live there for about a year. I was often very frightened because so many of my Muslim friends had been forced to leave or were killed. There were many times when they forced me to show three fingers. If I didn't they probably would have killed me. Once when I was in a nearby village called Jelah someone threw a grenade into a group of people because we didn't show the right sign. The shrapnel injured my shoulder very badly. This is why people here react to that sign. Many bad things have happened because of it."

I spent the next week preparing for Sarajevo. Nadina and her family were adjusting to the reality of moving to Canada. She had been dating a young Croatian man for about four months, and there was talk of getting married and allowing him to join her. I spent a good amount of time discussing this situation with Nadina. She was only twenty-one, too young for such a commitment. And yet marriage would give him the chance for a normal life. I was sure that in the end this is what she would choose. They would leave for Canada when I was in Sarajevo. Nadina and her family joined us at the bus late Sunday night. For all of us it would be the beginning of a wonderful adventure.

The bus arrived in Split, a city along the Adriatic Sea, early the next morning. A different bus company served Bosnia and we went to buy a ticket. A middle-aged woman unlocked the door at six o'clock and we went inside. Snjezana told her where we were going and the woman immediately looked concerned. She seemed to be explaining the danger of the trip. After several minutes of discussion Snjezana explained that we were willing to accept the risk, and paid for the tickets. When we walked outside she stopped me.

"I must tell you what the woman was saying," she said. "Yesterday the same bus to Sarajevo was attacked in Herzegovina. This has happened four times in the last two months. Two Croatian soldiers with automatic rifles stopped the bus and robbed everyone on board. They then shot the bus with machine guns and beat several of the people, including the driver. He is now in the hospital. They are warning everyone about the danger. Many people have decided not to go. I told her that we would continue."

"Why would Croatian soldiers attack the bus?" I asked.

"Herzegovina is very poor. It is also very Croatian. They consider themselves part of Croatia. Many times people are bringing cash to relatives in Bosnia and are robbed. Now that the war is over people are trying to rebuild their lives. The people in this part are very primitive and racist. She is not exaggerating when she says it is dangerous."

The journey to Sarajevo had begun and I was wondering if we had made the right decision. I had been waiting for this opportunity for a long time. It was too late to turn back. Regardless of the risk, I knew I had to finish it. Something was waiting for me, some grand finale that I was sure Teacher was behind. The anticipation made any risk acceptable.

The trip from Split to Sarajevo took eight hours. I was amazed at the beautiful mountains and lakes that defined Bosnia's landscape. As we crossed into Herzegovina, the reality of the situation became clear. The contrast between the beauty of the country and the devastation of war was dramatic. We passed entire villages that were completely destroyed. In some cases it was clear that many homes were destroyed only because the owners were Muslim. One house was completely demolished while only a few feet away the next was hardly touched. For four hundred and fifty years, people of different religions lived side by side in Bosnia. The intolerance brought on by the war made this impossible now.

The bus pulled into Mostar, a city in Herzegovina that was evenly divided between Muslims and Catholics. The devastation was unimaginable. The Muslim area was in ruin. Nearly half the buildings were either completely destroyed or were empty shells. People wandered through the streets with empty, lost eyes. Tanks and soldiers were everywhere. It was a city paralyzed, shaken to the very core by violence most people cannot even imagine. The destruction of Mostar was not at the hands of the Serbs but the Croatian Catholics. It was a war over who would control the city. Croatian soldiers were brought in to conduct the massacre. The Muslim people, without weapons or defenses, were completely crushed.

We passed one village after another that was abandoned and destroyed. Buildings were riddled with bullets and huge round shell holes. The bus hummed with nervous excitement. Some people seemed to be returning to their homes while others, like Snjezana and me, were traveling to Bosnia as part of various humanitarian efforts. I met three German filmmakers who were trying to establish an Internet link to transmit photos from Bosnia. Two men from England were on their way to a town where they had been working with young people for more than two years. Each time we passed a village, our cameras were out and waiting for the shot that would portray the reality of the situation. Of course none of them could. No picture or television report I had ever seen could have prepared me for what I was seeing.

Sarajevo is surrounded by steep hills, all occupied by Bosnian Serbs. Controlling the fate of Sarajevo during the war was easy. Block all roads leading in or out of the city and you had it by the throat. Without the intervention of Europe and the United States, Sarajevo had no chance of survival. For four years the cannons and snipers sat on the hills picking off civilians one by one. More than fifteen thousand people were killed in

Sarajevo during the war. Fifty thousand more were injured.

As the bus approached the Serbian suburbs of Sarajevo, we were joined by five IFOR tanks, which escorted us into the city. The French Army controlled this region. The U.S. Army was west of Sarajevo in Tusla. Three tanks led the convoy, with two more behind us. This was common procedure since IFOR, the acronym for the unified NATO Army, took over the area to implement the peace accord. The Serbian villages were quiet. There seemed to be very little destruction in this area. It wasn't until we crossed the line that divided these two cultures that I understood what had happened here. The main road that led into Sarajevo was lined with tall apartment and office buildings, nearly all of which were destroyed. It looked like the Oklahoma City bombing times fifty. For every ten cars there were three tanks or military vehicles. Soldiers with automatic weapons were everywhere. We had entered a war zone, there was no way to deny that fact.

We were met at the bus station by Harris, a friend from Rijeka who had just moved back to Sarajevo with his mother. His grandmother was in the hospital and they offered us her apartment. It was in a ten-story building in a complex of several other identical buildings. At least two of the buildings had been partially or completely destroyed. The apartment complex was at the base of the hill that led to the Serbian villages, easy targets for the grenade launchers. The wind was cold and the ground was covered with snow. During most of the war the city was without gas or water. This meant that many homes were without heat and the only source of water was a nearby pump. Since the Serbs knew the location of these pumps, many people were killed in this way. But things were much better now. Water was available about ten hours a day and gas perhaps twelve. For them this was the sign that their lives were returning to normal. For me it meant limited showers and freezing nights.

It was already late in the afternoon. Josip Pejakovic would meet us at the apartment at seven o'clock and we would begin arranging the itinerary. I learned that Josip was a great celebrity in the former Yugoslavia. For thirty years he was the leading man in the National Theater in Sarajevo. He had also starred in many movies as well as a popular television series. But his politics were always radically different from that of his comrades. While the masses were moving toward nationalism he promoted a unified Bosnia, one where each culture lived in peace just as they had for hundreds of years. He was the alternative candidate for the Bosnian presidency immediately preceding the war. He spoke out against nationalism and religious separatism, a decision that made him very unpopular once the war began. In fact, Sarajevo is one of the only cities in the former Yugoslavia where he is safe. Once, while visiting Mostar, he was forced to leave in the middle of the night when he learned of a plot to assassinate him. He abandoned acting and politics and devoted himself to relieving the plight of Sarajevo.

Josip was often referred to as "Jesus of Sarajevo." When people were hungry he bought a truckload of bread and fed them. An orphanage for retarded children was built in the city and Josip bought their food for two years. His generosity was not limited to any one culture or religion. Dozens of Serbians who lived in the city once came to him because of extreme persecution. At that time gasoline cost the equivalent of fifty dollars per gallon. Josip found them cars and filled the gas tanks to help them escape. I wondered what to expect when I met this man.

The doorbell rang and Snjezana opened the door. A striking, huge man walked through the door. He was unshaven, his hair was not combed, and his clothes were modest and old. Snjezana led him into the living room and introduced me to him.

"It is a great pleasure to meet a Peace Troubadour," he said with a deep dramatic voice. "Sarajevo certainly needs more than one."

Snjezana asked him to sit down and offered him coffee. We chatted for a few minutes about various things, all unrelated to Sarajevo and my concert. Then he leaned forward and became very serious.

"This has been a very dark time for my city," he said. "The grenades have stopped and we are able to walk down the street, but this war is still far from over. As long as people continue to separate themselves from one another the hatred will remain. We will not have lasting peace until we change the way we think. That is why we invited you,

Jimmy. Concerts like yours help us to realize all the ways we are the same, how each of us wants peace. I know that many people will come to your concert."

I was struck by how much Josip sounded like an Emissary, and yet as far as I knew he had nothing to do with them. He was friends with the poet who had originally contacted Snjezana about me performing in Sarajevo. No one knew what happened to the poet. He had apparently passed the responsibility over to Josip and that was the last Snjezana heard from him. Josip was the director of an interreligious peace organization in Sarajevo that was sponsoring the concert. The next day we had a meeting scheduled with the committee responsible for planning the city's winter festival. They would decide what theater the concert would be performed in. I was then scheduled to be interviewed on a local independent radio program.

"During the war the Serbs tried to crush the soul of this city," Josip explained. "They destroyed the library, music halls, and theaters, anything that represented Sarajevo's culture. We were once one of the greatest cultural cities in Europe. Our national theater was the envy of Yugoslavia. But now all that has changed. Your concert will be one of the first musical events here in nearly five years."

"When will you begin acting again?" Snjezana asked him.

"I will not act here again," he said. "There is nothing here for me now. The government is not interested in promoting great theater. Even if they were I would not appear on the stage. My dream is to bring my family to America. Perhaps there I can begin again. But how am I to go? It would be easy for me to declare political asylum but I will not. Those who oppose my politics cannot think they have beaten me. What I want is cultural asylum. What happens when you can no longer work at what you are famous for? I do not know if there is such a thing, but I will dream it nonetheless."

I knew from that first meeting that Josip was going to be an important part of this story. I felt like he was sent to us, or perhaps we were sent to him. Only time would tell.

After our meeting with the festival committee we drove to the radio station. On the way Josip pointed out many of the buildings that were destroyed during the war. The library was once one of the most beautiful buildings in Sarajevo. It was now an empty shell. Block after block was bombed and burned. I could see the pain in Josip's eyes as he pointed out each building. This was once a beautiful city, he often said. Now it was a frighteningly sad and oppressed place.

Studio 99, located in the basement of the government building, was the only independent radio station in Bosnia. As we walked through the halls it was interesting to see people's reaction to Josip. He was the Marlon Brando of Yugoslavia. People stopped to shake his hand and encouraged him to return to the stage. He was polite to them all, regardless of his own feelings. Everyone was aware when Josip entered the room. No one said a word to us as we walked through the waiting area to the studio.

We sat down in the largest studio. Microphones were adjusted and sound levels were set. It would be a live interview, conducted by the disc jockey working at the time. As we were settling in, a young woman walked in and sat down next to me.

"My name is Azra," she said as she held out her hand. "I will be your translator."

"It's nice to meet you," I said.

"Just please talk slowly and stop every ten seconds. If you get too far ahead I will not remember what you said." She smiled.

Seconds later the red light was on and the interview began. The disc jockey asked why I came to Bosnia, what I hoped to accomplish, and about the concert. With each question Azra looked deep into my eyes as if she was looking right through me. The music from the Peace Concert CD was playing in the background and I felt myself relaxing, not because of the music but because of Azra. There was something about her that stirred me in a strange and wonderful way. She was young, perhaps in her early twenties, with dark brown hair and the face of an angel. I paid little attention to the DJ asking the questions. I waited for Azra, listening to her translation, then speaking right to her, as if there was no one there but us.

"What is the main thing you hope to accomplish in Sarajevo?" the interviewer asked through Azra.

"I want to show people that there is no such thing as a religious war," I said. "Religion is always about peace, not war. Every religion teaches cooperation and pacifism.

To show this I am going to sing the Muslim and the Christian Peace Prayers together at the concert, showing their common purpose."

When the interview was over they played the remainder of the CD. I was happy to know that the peace prayers from the twelve religions of the world were floating through the airways of Sarajevo. Snjezana and Josip went into another room to discuss details of a television interview and I stayed in the office with Azra.

"How did you learn to speak English so well?" I asked her.

"No one believes me when I tell them that I have never studied English," she said. "I learned it on my own, mainly by watching American movies."

"You never studied English in school?"

"You see, you don't believe me either. I have watched hundreds of movies. Ever since I was a child I dreamed of living in America. When I watch American movies I almost feel like I am there."

"It's strange how many people I have met here that want to move to America," I told her.

"Most people in Sarajevo would move

nearly anywhere. You cannot imagine what it was like here during the war. We couldn't even walk down the street without being afraid of the snipers. Once, very late at night, I wanted to see the stars. It had been so long and I wanted to see them just for a minute. My mother didn't know where I was. She would have been very angry if she knew I was sitting on our front steps. Suddenly I heard a pop far away in the distance, then the sound of a bullet fly by my ear. It was no more than ten centimeters from my head. I fell on the ground and acted like I was dead. I was so afraid that I couldn't even move. The thought of someone on a hill looking at me through the telescope of a rifle paralyzed me. I finally stood up and ran into the house. No one in my family ever knew about this. I was too afraid to tell them."

Azra's story touched me very deeply. Most people I met in Sarajevo seemed cut off from the outside world, as if they had drawn the curtains and lived within themselves. I sensed a bright light in Azra, as if she had been able to remain herself regardless of how frightening the war had been. I wanted to help her. She had very little chance of living the life she deserved in Sarajevo. Nadina found a way to get to Canada. Perhaps there was a way for Azra as well.

Just then Josip and Snjezana walked into the room. They looked very serious, especially Snjezana. They sat down on the couch across from me.

"There is something I must tell you," Josip said. "Things are still very tense in Bosnia. People are still not able to release the hatred they feel toward one another. This idea of singing the Muslim and the Christian Peace Prayers together is quite radical. This has never been done before in Sarajevo and many people will not like it. Five minutes ago, as soon as the interview had ended, there was a phone call. A man said to tell you that if you sing the peace prayers together you would be assassinated. I am afraid we will have to take this threat very seriously. We need to discuss alternatives."

"Alternatives to what?" I asked.

"Maybe you shouldn't sing the prayers," Snjezana said. "You can sing the other peace songs and that will be enough. There is no need to put yourself in danger."

I stood up and walked to the other side of

the room. "So you think they really might try to kill me."

"People do not make idle threats in Sarajevo," Josip said. "When someone says he is going to kill you, he means it."

"But I didn't come here for a vacation," I said. "I was aware of the risks before I came. I knew it was dangerous. The fact that my singing these prayers has stirred such passion is all the more reason to do it."

"You didn't come here to get killed," Snjezana said. "That would serve no purpose at all."

"You're right, I didn't come here to get killed. And I won't. There is something else happening here, something beyond all of this. You know that, Snjezana. I must sing the prayers together, regardless of the risk."

Azra sat and listened. I knew in that instant that she had been drawn into the story, just like the rest of us. Duro said that the final lesson would come in Sarajevo. Perhaps this was it. I knew that I had to sing the peace songs. I didn't know what was going to happen but I had already come through so much. I had to trust that Teacher knew what he was doing. Even though he was gone I believed he was still orchestrating this drama.

Over the next two days I spent as much time as I could with Azra. She showed me around Sarajevo, introduced me to her friends, and gave me a clear picture of what life was like during the war. In the evening we walked through downtown Sarajevo as if it was any other city, watching the people, sitting in cafés, and getting to know each other. I had no idea what Sarajevo would be like. Everything I had heard led me to believe it was dangerous to even step outside. And yet, everyone seemed anxious to begin living normal lives, the lives they had been robbed of for four years. The young people were no different than young people anywhere. Most spoke adequate English and were excited to talk to me about their lives. The most common thing I heard was that they felt they had been robbed of so much. It's impossible to be young during a war. Each day is so uncertain and the pressure is so great. Now that there was peace they were ready to remember what it is like to be alive.

"I've never had what I would call a true friend," she told me as we sat in a café.

"During the war we were all so concentrated on surviving that it was hard to think of others. I did have one friend who I spent most of my time with, but then something happened. She decided not to be my friend anymore, just like that. I have no idea why. Now people are trying to get back to the way things were. And yet, they're still afraid. I've been keeping my own feelings inside so long that I thought I had lost the ability to care. But I haven't. Meeting you has meant so much to me. I believe that you will be my real friend, and that makes me very happy."

I reached over and took her hand. "I have the same feeling, Azra. Ever since I first came to Croatia last summer my life has been guided. I have met so many people that are now important parts of my life. And that is how I feel about you. Even though we just met, and we live such different lives, I know you are now part of this story, part of the whole wonderful adventure I've been on. I don't know how or why, but I know it's true. I'm going to do whatever I can to get you to the United States. You deserve the chance at a normal life. There are so many scars here in Sarajevo. It could take a long time for people to let go of their pain. If nothing else, I believe we met so that you'll have a chance. From there . . . who knows."

The concert was scheduled for the next evening. Josip had booked a theater in the center of the city that was once the most popular theater in Yugoslavia. Thanks to Josip, word had gone out in a big way. Local and national television crews were coming to videotape the concert. It would be aired on national television in its entirety and the local station would feature portions of the concert as well as an interview as part of a weekly program on peace. Josip invited everyone he knew. The director of the National Theater and a famous European movie director would both attend. The concert was becoming a bigger event than I had imagined, and the fact that I planned to sing the Muslim and Christian Peace Prayers gained a lot of attention. I thought about the death threat. Though I was confident about my decision, I had to wonder. I didn't want to take unnecessary risks for the sake of a dramatic ending to the book. What about my daughter? There was more to this decision than I had first thought.

The theater was nearly full when I arrived. Snjezana and Josip were waiting for me backstage, and Azra was in my dressing room with a crew from the local television station. There was just enough time to do the interview before the concert. Afterward I waited backstage with Josip. He seemed anxious, worried for me. I was sure that nothing would happen during the performance. Perhaps it was just a threat made by an extremist with no intention of actually following through. Snjezana had been trying to make me reconsider my decision for two days. Now it was too late. Josip walked onstage and introduced me.

I walked onto the stage amid great applause. The spotlight made seeing the audience impossible. I sat down on the stool and played a medley of three songs: Marvin Gaye's "What's Going On," and John Lennon's "Imagine" and "All We Are Saying . . ." Then I set the guitar on the ground.

"Last summer I was riding a tram in Zagreb and I began to sing a song in my head. When I arrived at my stop I found a pen so I could write it down. It was called 'Let's Put an End to War.' Since then a poet in Rijeka arranged the lyrics to your language and I'm going to try and sing at least part of it tonight. Then I'll sing it in English just in case you don't understand my bad Croatian. A couple of weeks after I wrote that song I found myself in the mountains of Croatia with a secret spiritual community called the Emissaries of Light. They told me that humanity had evolved to the point that it was ready to finally accept peace. They said that we were on the verge of a great spiritual shift away from the destruction of war to the harmony of peace. It is interesting that I wrote this song just before meeting these people. It seems to exemplify everything they believe, and I'd like to share it with you now."

I picked the guitar up off the floor and began to play.

I had a dream last night.
All the people in the world were
involved.
It seemed the earth had evolved to the
point
Where we put an end to war.

I said a prayer last night.
It filled my heart with such resolve.
No longer would I involve my mind
With empty thoughts of war.

Between the night and tomorrow
A great thing did occur.
Between the cries and the sorrow
I could almost hear these words:
"Let's put an end to war.
It's peace we're living for.
Let's put an end to war."

I heard a voice last night.
The voice was soft but oh so strong.
It whispered, "How long, how long
Will you put your faith in war?"

I had a dream last night.
Not a country or place remained
With bombs or guns or fighter planes,
'Cause we'd put an end to war.

And in the dark forbidding sky
A great sign did appear.
The sound of joy and laughter
Did fill the air.
'Cause we'd put an end to war.
It's love we're living for.
Let's put an end to war.

The concert was a great success. I had finally performed the Peace Concert in Sarajevo, with the Muslim and Christian Peace Prayers. Azra was there waiting for me backstage. She had been there through the entire concert.

"You were fantastic," she said as she threw her arms around me. "I'm so glad I was alone so no one would see me crying."

"I'm just glad it's finally over," I said.

"What will you do now?"

"I don't know. I guess we'll be leaving tomorrow. Josip arranged another concert in Mostar."

"No, I mean right now. What are you doing after you leave the theater?"

Just then the back door to the theater opened and a man walked through. I couldn't see him well, only that he was tall and thin. He walked over to us.

"I was sent to bring you to a restaurant for a celebration party," he said in English. "The car is here in the alley."

"Well, I guess that answers that question," I said to Azra. "Why don't you join us."

"That would be great," she said.

I looked back at the man. "Hold on for one minute while I go and get my guitar."

Just then something happened. He had

stepped into the light and I could see into his eyes. I felt something inside me. It was intense fear. He was sent to kill me, I was sure of it. I could read his mind, just like Toni taught me. His eyes were cold and dark. If we got into that car with him we were dead. I took Azra's hand and told her to come help me. I walked onto the stage and grabbed the guitar.

"What's wrong?" Azra asked.

"Just come with me and don't say anything," I whispered.

We jumped off the stage and ran to the front entrance. There were still many people waiting and we were immediately surrounded. I saw Snjezana and Josip near the door. I thought about running to them but I knew we were safe as long as there were people around. Just then I felt someone squeeze my arm.

"Come with me, quickly," he whispered in my ear. I looked into his eyes. They were soft and bright. Just as I knew I was in danger with the other man I knew we were safe with him. I excused myself and grabbed Azra's arm. We darted through a side entrance to a car that was already running.

"Quickly, get into the back," he said as he got behind the wheel. Azra got in, then I handed her the guitar. The car pulled away just as I closed the door.

"Where are you taking us?" I asked the man.

"Somewhere safe," he said. "Perhaps you don't know this but you were nearly killed tonight. There were people in the theater with orders to assassinate you."

"But why would anyone want to kill me just because I sang a couple of peace songs?"

"It's more than that. Killing you also serves a political motive as well. We are aware that many people in America don't believe your army should be in Bosnia. If a few people like you were killed there would be great pressure on your president to pull the troops out. If the Americans leave so do the European forces. The peace accord would fall apart and things would be as they were before. This is what the radical National groups here want. You were just a means to an end."

"And who are you?"

"My name is Robert. I am the person who invited you to come to Sarajevo."

"You're the poet. I was wondering what happened to you. How did you know we were in trouble?"

"That is not something I can explain just yet. For now sit back and relax. We will be there in a few minutes."

I wondered where "there" was. I looked over at Azra. She seemed to be enjoying the excitement. Everything had happened so fast, I didn't know what to think. The car crossed the river that led to the hill. If we continued in this direction we would soon be in the Serbian part of town. A few seconds later he turned down an alley and stopped behind a building. Robert got out of the car and opened the back door. He took the guitar and motioned for us to follow him.

We walked between two buildings toward a door with a dim light above it. Robert unlocked the door and held it open for us. Azra and I waited for him inside. He then led us down a wide hallway and into a room on the left. He turned on the light, asked us to sit down, then left. The room looked like some sort of a waiting area. Chairs were set against the wall and a single small desk sat in one corner. We took our coats off and sat down.

"Do you have any idea where we are?" I asked Azra.

"I don't know this area of the city very well," she said. "It is very dangerous because it is so close to the Serbian section."

Just then the door opened and Robert walked into the room. He held the door for the man behind him. When I saw who it was I nearly fainted.

"Welcome to Sarajevo," Toni, my attendant friend from the Emissaries, said.

I threw my arms around him. "Oh my God, Toni. I can't believe it's you."

"I've been watching you ever since you arrived here," he said. "Robert invited you because I asked him to."

"But what about the Emissaries? I went to the community with Duro and everyone was gone."

He motioned for all of us to sit down. "You shouldn't have been surprised to find the community empty. You are the reason for it being so. You learned about the Emissaries and have now begun teaching the world about them. Humanity has taken a new step, and the Emissaries are not needed in the way they have always been. Through your book people will learn to extend Divine

Light themselves, dramatically speeding up a new era."

"But what happened to them?"

"How can I explain this?" he said. "They are simply gone. Divine Light took them. This is ultimately what will happen to all of us. They didn't die, they ascended. One day something happened in session that had never happened before. It was as if the Light reversed itself. Instead of it extending out of the wheel, it came in. As it did, everything within the wheel began to glow and spin. Then suddenly, there was a brilliant flash of light and when we looked they were gone. The Emissaries and the wheel had vanished. We all knew what had happened. They had been preparing us for that day for weeks, almost as soon as you left. We knew it was over, or actually, that it had just begun. The attendants all went their separate ways, some back to their homes and others to places where they can continue their work. I came here to Sarajevo. This is where I will plant the seeds of peace, or extend everything I learned from the Emissaries."

"What is this place?" I asked him.

"This is the only place in Bosnia where people of every religion and culture are living together in peace. This is the beginning, the model that will teach others how to live."

Just then there was a knock on the door. Robert walked over and opened it. A young boy stood holding a tray with cups filled with coffee. He was perhaps ten years old and his head appeared to have suffered some sort of trauma. It had huge long scars running in two directions with a slight indentation on one side. He said something to Robert, then handed him the tray. The child was obviously retarded, probably from the injury to his head. He walked over to Toni and sat down on his lap.

"This is Damian," Toni said. "He lives here with us. He is a member of our community. During the war his parents were killed and he was badly injured. He is Bosnian, but there are also Serbs and Croats living here as well. There is no difference among them. We live together in peace."

"Where are the other community members?" I asked.

"They are all sleeping. Damian never goes to sleep until very late so he stays with me. The others go to bed around eight o'clock."

"Wait a minute," I said. "Are you telling

me that this is a home for retarded children? This is your spiritual community?"

"That's correct. This is a home for children who are mentally disabled and orphaned. This is where we begin. Like I said, it is the only place in Bosnia where people of every culture are living together. These children are a sign, one so subtle and innocent that it is hard to notice. To me they are no different than any other group committed to peace. From this little seed an entire new culture will be born here in Sarajevo. This is what I came to do. I wanted you to see it so you would understand."

"Understand what?"

"That we can't judge by appearances. Look at this city. Everywhere is the destruction of war. Hatred seems to have had its way. But is that true? If you learned anything from the Emissaries you will know that it isn't. This is the result of a world bent on proving that separation is real. Only love is real, no matter how things appear. The role of an Emissary is to look past the illusion to the truth, to literally look through the world. This is true forgiveness, and it is what will bring a new, true vision of the world to humanity. This is the final lesson. Without forgiveness everything you have learned is incomplete. When you learn to see past the effects of the world to the true cause, then you will be able to extend lasting peace."

There was a knock on the door. When Robert opened it Josip and Snjezana walked in and sat down. Everything made sense. Josip had been part of this mystery from the very beginning. He knew all about Teacher and the other Emissaries. Toni had arranged it all, from inviting me to Sarajevo to introducing me to Josip. The only thing that they had not planned for was the death threat. And yet Toni still knew to send Robert to save us, narrowly escaping what would have been a tragedy. Snjezana and I stayed at the orphanage that night, in case whoever it was that was trying to kill me was waiting for us at the apartment. I was so happy to see Toni again. The pieces all fit together now, all the lessons I learned from Teacher to the mystery behind my invitation to Sarajevo. We sat up for several hours talking about the Emissaries and everything that had happened. At midnight Robert told Azra he would give her a ride home. Before she left I asked her to step outside with me.

"We'll be leaving tomorrow," I told her. "Josip has arranged a concert in Mostar. I just wanted you to know how much being with you the past few days has meant to me."

"And you will never know how much it meant to me. Just because you're leaving doesn't mean we'll be apart. You are my true friend. That's all that is important. I believe that I will come to America someday. And when I do we will see each other again."

"I'm going to do whatever I can to get you there," I said. "I feel such tenderness for you, Azra. One way or another we will be together again."

I held her in my arms until Robert came to bring her home, then stood there in the alley watching as the car pulled away. I knew it wouldn't be the last time I would see Azra. She was part of the bigger story that had only just begun.

Early the next morning Josip called the organization that was sponsoring my concert in Mostar. Things had changed dramatically. More than a hundred Croatian special police had been brought in the day before anticipating renewed violence between the Catholics and the Muslims. All foreigners had been evacuated and buses were being detoured around the city. The concert was canceled.

Snjezana and I decided to return to Rijeka. It was too dangerous for me to remain in Sarajevo, and I had already more than accomplished all of my goals. Josip drove us to the bus station and we said goodbye. I felt so blessed to have met him and so many others in Sarajevo. The city's spirit had not been crushed. Through the inspiration of people like Josip, Toni, and Robert, I was sure Sarajevo would rise again.

As we approached the Serbian sector we were once again met by the column of tanks that escorted us safely through the mountains. The trip had ended. I couldn't believe so much had happened, not only since I arrived in Bosnia, but since I originally thought the book was finished. This had to be the finale. It was the perfect ending. I sat back in my seat and took a deep breath, grateful that I had been guided safely through this adventure.

When the bus was within several kilometers of Mostar it turned down a small road to the left. The detour would take us a good distance away from the normal route and add about an hour to our trip. We rode past one small village after another. We were in Herzegovina, an area that considered itself Croatian, despite the fact that it was actually in Bosnia. This seemed to be the main problem. Religion had been woven together with nationalism so tightly that there was very little tolerance for anyone or anything that did not fit neatly into the established way of things. It didn't seem to matter where you lived. If you were Catholic you were Croatian, pure and simple.

I was looking out the window when the bus pulled into a small village. Snjezana had fallen asleep. The driver turned the engine off and announced that we would take a fifteen-minute break. I woke Snjezana up and asked her if she wanted anything to eat. She sat up in the seat and asked where we were. I didn't know. When we got off the bus Snjezana asked the driver.

"We're in Medjugorje," she said, "that place where Mary is supposed to be appearing to six children."

I couldn't believe my ears. "We have to

stay," I told her. "There's no way I'm going to miss a chance to spend time in Medjugorje. It's no accident that we're here."

Snjezana found out that another bus would pass through town at six o'clock the next evening. It was no problem to leave this bus and reboard then. We took our things from the luggage compartment and began walking toward the little village. At the end of the street I could see a huge white church with two tall steeples. On each side were modern restaurants and souvenir stores. A few years ago Medjugorje was nothing more than a few unpaved roads and houses. Millions of people had come since the apparitions began, creating a thriving tourist industry. Many families had added additions onto their homes to accommodate these seekers. Along the main road there were at least ten different shops all selling the same rosaries, plastic statues of Mary, and holy cards.

We walked to the church at the end of the road. This was the center of activity in Medjugorje, the place where the daily apparitions took place after government officials banned gatherings on the nearby hill where the apparitions began. Several of the children were married and had moved from Medjugorje but were still being visited by Mary every day at 5:45 in the afternoon, wherever they happened to be. When we arrived in the church it was half full. We put our luggage against the wall and sat down in the back. They were praying the rosary in Croatian. I was surprised to see so many young people there. The apparitions had sparked a renewal of faith in everyone, including the young.

I felt a tremendous amount of energy all around me, a feeling similar to what I experienced with the Emissaries. I closed my eyes and began to meditate. Almost immediately I felt myself beginning to vibrate, just as I had the last day of session. The feeling was intense but pleasant. The sound of the people praying resonated deep within me. I began to remember everything Teacher told me about Medjugorje, that there was a great resurgence of Divine Light in this place. What the children were experiencing was real, he said, regardless of the decidedly Catholic tone. I could feel the energy moving through and around me. After some time Snjezana touched me on the arm and motioned it was time to go.

We found a boardinghouse and rented two rooms. There was only one other person staying there at the time, a man from France who seemed eager to talk even though he spoke no English. The building was unheated, something I had grown used to since arriving in the area. I had not spent a single night in a warm bedroom. And yet the excitement of being in Medjugorje overshadowed everything. I had a feeling that something incredible was going to happen the next day. Every time I thought the book had ended something else happened that gave it a new direction. I finally relaxed and fell asleep, wondering what was next.

I was awakened by the sound of a rooster just outside my window. It was six o'clock and the farm was alive with activity. I tried to go back to sleep but couldn't. Snjezana was already up and was having coffee with the family who owned the boardinghouse. They invited me to join them. After breakfast we walked back to the church to see what was scheduled that day. English Mass was at noon. There were also several guided tours to the top of Apparition Hill. We walked around the village for a couple of hours, then decided to join one of the tours. As we stood near the entrance of the church waiting for the tour to begin, I noticed a small round hill in the opposite direction of Apparition Hill. I had a strange feeling of being drawn to it, as if it were a magnet. I looked at it for a long time but saw nothing unusual. It was calling me, I was sure of it. When the others arrived for the tour I told Snjezana to go on without me. I would meet her at noon.

I began walking through the fields that led to the hill. It looked like it was only a ten- or fifteen-minute walk away. I walked through the fields and vineyards for nearly an hour before I arrived at the base. I came to a tiny village. There didn't seem to be a path that led up the hill, so I walked over to a young man standing in front of a small hut. He didn't speak English but I was able to tell him I wanted to go to the top of the hill. He motioned for me to follow him. He would show me the way.

Climbing the hill was extremely difficult. Constant attention needed to be paid to the loose rocks to avoid being injured from a fall. The hill was also covered with thick thorn-bushes. Before long my hands and arms were bleeding from the scratches. My guide led me up halfway, then motioned for me to continue straight. He didn't seem to understand why I would want to climb such a dangerous hill. I wasn't able to explain but I knew I must. There was something waiting for me at the top, that was all I knew.

I looked up to the crest of the hill and thought I saw something glowing. It was a bright day and I decided it was a trick of the sun. I continued to climb. I kept a close eye on the rocks and began to realize that each one had a design on it. I stopped to take a closer look. They were symbols, the same symbols that made up the wheel at the Emissary community. There were hundreds of small wheels and figure eights. I leaned over to feel the texture of the symbols and realized that they weren't drawn or carved on the rocks. It was almost as if they grew there by themselves. The lines were jagged and sometimes obscure, made of a dark, raised substance that felt like the rock itself. I looked to the top again. I was sure something was there, glowing and drawing me. I began to climb as fast as I could, led by a mysterious force. Before I knew it I was nearly there.

I noticed a huge pile of rocks at the very top of the hill. This was the spot that seemed to be glowing. The higher I went the more rocks had the obscure symbols. When I finally reached the top I looked again at the huge pile. It was twenty or thirty yards in front of me. I could see the light clearly now, and I couldn't believe my eyes. At the top was another small pile, about the size of a seat. Sitting at the very top was Teacher. He was sitting with his legs crossed and his eyes closed. The Light was all around him as if it were radiating from within.

When I got to the base of the pile of rocks I knelt down. I felt myself filled with energy, the same energy that was all around Teacher. He opened his eyes and looked at me.

"Don't be afraid," he said. "Come up here to the top."

The pile was about eight feet high. I climbed to the very top and sat down about seven feet away from him. I was now within the Light. Everything else seemed to disappear, as if we were floating high in a cloud. I was so happy to see him again. I thought that I would never have this chance again. He looked at me with such love and tenderness.

"I could never really leave you," he said.

"Now I can help you in ways that I couldn't before. Just because my body is gone doesn't mean that I'm not with you. I'll always be with you because you have begun the journey of becoming an Emissary."

It seemed as if his body wasn't actually touching the rocks but floating about an inch above them. I also had the strange feeling that he wasn't there at all, at least not in the physical way I was used to. I was looking at some sort of a projection, and yet he was only a few feet away from me.

"Where did you go?" I asked him. "I went back to the community with Duro and no one was there."

"Why did that surprise you? As Duro said, our work was finished almost as soon as you left. You've already begun to tell the world about the Emissaries. Humanity has begun to make the shift to the next level of evolution, the level we have prepared it for. Your work is now the important thing, not ours. It's through you that they will understand who they are."

"And why are you here with me now?"

"Because there's still one last thing I must show you. When you were in Sarajevo you learned how to look past the situation, the trauma and destruction, to the truth, which is unchanged. That is the way you brought peace to them, by showing them a true vision of themselves. The last thing I will show you is very personal. It is a Door to Eternity, the door you must step through before you can assume your role as a true Emissary. It is the passageway that separates this world from the real world, a tiny bridge that spans the gap between truth and illusion. Once you have walked through that door, stepped out of time and then come back, only then will you be able to fully complete your mission."

"And what is my mission?" I asked.

"To initiate a new group of Emissaries. The old one has fallen away. We are no longer needed. This new group will exist in a way that we couldn't have. Thousands of people just like you will take this step and become examples for the world. You will do this by existing outside the world and within it at the same time. Humanity will see the way you exist and learn from your example. Your commitment to exist outside of time will enliven a new group of Emissaries that will pave the way for the rest of humanity. The world has finally begun making the choice for peace. These new Emissaries will nurture that choice, helping all those to mature and extend this new vision of reality."

"What is the Door to Eternity?"

"It is an entryway to truth that has been right in front of you all along. As a human being you exist in a three-dimensional universe. And yet there are other dimensions of which you are completely unaware but that you have the ability to access. This is what a true Emissary does, move between these different dimensions. There is literally a door that is always directly in front of you. You need to learn to sense and actually see the door, then put your attention on it. The more attention you give it the more energy you will receive from it. And then it will pull you through it, all of you. It will pull you to the fourth dimension, a dimension beyond time and space, what you might call the causal level of existence. It is here that you will truly experience Divine Light, the source of creation. And then you will step back, back to the physical universe, and yet you will bring something of the fourth dimension back with you. This is what you will share. This is the gift an Emissary gives to the world."

"You're telling me that I will step through the door physically? You mean I will actually step into a whole new world?"

"You are the one who thinks your body and your spirit are separate. I said that you will step through the door completely, every element of your being. This includes your physical body. Even it must be transformed by the Light. When you do step through the door you may decide not to come back. There is nothing wrong with that decision, but you must remember that you chose to become an Emissary, and an Emissary always comes back. They are the link between the two worlds, the world of illusions and the real world. You and those who come after you will be like a signal to the rest of humanity. You will show them the way, just like I showed you the way.

"You must step through the Door to Eternity, the door that leads away from time. This is the step that all other lessons have led to. It begins with the release of fear, then sees past the illusion of separation. Once you have allowed Divine Light to build within you and permeate your being, only then are you ready to see the Door. All it takes is a shift in perception to see it."

"How can I learn to see the Door to Eternity?" I asked.

"Your desire will show it to you. I can help you focus your attention on the Door, but it is your desire to see it and step through it that reveals the passage to the fourth dimension."

Teacher asked me to sit down and close my eyes. He then led me through the meditation I learned when we were still with the Emissaries. I pulled my emotions together and projected them through my heart. My entire body was filled with an amazing energy. The symbols on the rocks seemed to change the air. The energy flooded from my heart and filled the area with Light.

"Now I want you to focus your attention about ten feet in front of you. Don't focus on anything in particular, just allow your gaze to hover in empty space. Now allow the Light that is being projected from your heart to fill that empty space. Don't try to see the Door with your eyes at first, but use your intuition and emotions. It is right in front of you. You just need to allow it to come into focus. You will begin to notice that the Light that is coming from your chest is disappearing in the area you are focusing on. It is actually being pulled into the Door. As this happens you will feel yourself expanding. It will happen slowly, but as you allow the energy to build you will begin to see an opening—not a physical opening, but one that exists beyond the physical. It is a new dimension, the entryway to a new level of existence."

As he spoke I began to sense something like a door or an opening hovering about ten feet in front of me. I couldn't see it with my eyes but I did feel it. The Light coming from my heart began to disappear in the area of the opening. After about a minute something began to change. I could see something forming, almost like a piece of clear plastic floating in space. The Light was hitting the opening and then disappearing as if it were being sucked in. I felt myself wanting to go to the Door. Seeing it filled me with incredible peace and joy, and I wanted to see where it led.

"Allow the Door to take you," Teacher said. "The Light you are projecting into the Door is like a rope that pulls you closer. Let it pull you out of time to eternity. Let your desire grow strong and increase until you feel you must go to it. The Light will pull you. Just let yourself be taken."

I felt myself being sucked into the Door. Everything around me began to fade and my mind did not operate as it normally did. I was totally at peace, yet filled with an incredible energy. I didn't know if my body was moving or not. All I knew was that my essence was being pulled forward, as if this was the fulfillment of my whole life, to step out of time. I was floating through space, moving slowly toward the Door. As I did I could see through it, as if the whole universe were on the other side. If I stepped through I knew the world would disappear. Everything I knew would be gone.

Suddenly I was moving backward, back into my body. I was afraid, and with that thought the Door to Eternity began to disappear. A few seconds later I was aware of my surroundings, the rock I was sitting on, and Teacher still sitting in front of me.

"What happened?" I asked him, disappointed that I was back.

"Fear is what happened. You were afraid of what would happen if you stepped outside of time. Just for an instant you believed that everything you know would disappear forever, as if everything you love would be gone. Fear is the only thing that keeps you from seeing the Door to Eternity. It doesn't surprise me that this happened. I would have been amazed if you were able to step through so quickly. Just being aware of the Door is a major step. That alone is a great accomplishment."

"Will I be able to see the Door again?"

"Look in front of you and see if you can see it."

I took a deep breath and let my gaze hover where I saw the Door before. Within a few seconds I could see it, just as it had been. Once again I felt the incredible peace of being aware of the Door to Eternity.

"When you've seen the Door once, you will always be able to see it again," Teacher said. "You just need to know how to look. You've trained your eyes not to see it. But you can relearn and discover what has always been right in front of your eyes. Stepping through the Door is something that will happen on its own when you have completely released your fear. You will step out of time and experience eternity, then you will step back as an Emissary of Light. I have taught you everything I can about this. There is another who is coming to you. He will be the one who will take you to the next level."

"What do you mean?" I asked. "Do you mean that I will have another teacher? Where will you be?"

"I'll be right where I have always been—within you. I cannot tell you anything more about the one who will come, only that you need him and he can help you. All I will say is this: You must be diligent and focus your mind on one thing—stepping through the Door of Eternity. This must be your single goal. Nothing else matters but this."

The light around Teacher's body began to grow brighter until it was hard to see him. It was as if he was being taken by the Light, or going through the Door himself.

"Remember, Jimmy, there is no death. I did not die, and regardless of how you perceive your body, only life is real. Tell everybody what you have seen. Help them to understand how holy they are, that they are all Emissaries of Light. Humanity has taken an incredible step, and with that step comes new responsibilities. Help them put down their toys and accept peace where it really is—within. I am always with you, Jimmy. Never forget that."

Suddenly he was gone. The light vanished and I was sitting alone at the top of the hill. I closed my eyes and took a deep breath. I felt a sense of peace that I had never felt before, a feeling of certainty that everything was in perfect order. I sat there for a very long time. Then I stood up, looked around me, and walked down the hill.

Peace Organizations

Action Council for
Peace in the
Balkans
P.O. Box 28268
Washington, D.C.
20038–0268 USA
(202) 737–1414
email:
ActionCncl@aol.com

American Friends
Service Committee
2161
Massachusetts
Avenue
Cambridge, MA
02140 USA
(617) 661–6130

Amnesty
International
322 Eighth Avenue
NY, NY 10001 USA
(212) 807–8400
email:
aiaction@igc.apc.org

Balkan Institute
P.O. Box 27974
Washington, D.C.
20038–7974 USA
(202) 737–5219
email:
BalkanInst@aol.com

Commissione Di
Giustizia, Pace E
Salvaguardia Del
Creato
Piazzetta S.
Spagnoli, 1
06081 Assisi (PG)
Italia
Tel. 39–(0) 75–
815194
Fax 39–(0) 75–
815197

Nonviolence
International
P.O. Box 39127
Friendship Station,
N.W.

Washington, D.C.
20016 USA
(202) 244–0951
email:
nonviolence@
igc.apc.org

Rijeka Suncokret
(Rijeka Sunflower)
Kumiciceva 33a
51000 Rijeka,
Croatia
Tel./Fax 385–
5142369

Sri Chinmoy
Peace Runs
International
61–20 Grand
Central Parkway,
Suite B–408
Forest Hills, NY
11375 USA
Tel. (718) 760–
0250
Fax (718) 592–
1696

The Peace Abbey
Two North Main
Street
Sherborn, MA
01770 USA
Tel. (508) 650–
3659
Fax (508) 655–
5031

Peace Online
Network
(PeaceNet): for
more information
send a blank email
message to:
peacenet–
info@peacenet.apc.
org

Author's Note

For information on James Twyman's Peace Concert CD, his schedule of concerts and workshops, or the Emissary of Light Newsletter, please send a self-addressed stamped envelope to:

Emissary of Light Newsletter
P.O. Box 397
Accord, Massachusetts 02018